"Several years ago I heard Dee Duke tell t   .on in his
life and t■he church he pastors. God move(—prayer
is not just a priority, it is *the* priority. No   l the hard
way and breaks new ground by applying them to ...   follower of
Christ. This practical study will challenge and motivate anyone who seeks deeper intimacy
with God _ "

Dr. Don Wiggins
Vice President for National Church Ministries
The Christian & Missionary Alliance

"Prayer is work. This book gives you the tools to leverage your effectiveness, thirty, sixty and
one hundred fold."

Nelson Malwitz
President, Finishers Project

"Dee Duke's book takes prayer beyond a discipline and shows us how to create a lifestyle of
prayer that can dramatically change our lives and the lives of men and women around us."

Merrill Oster
President, Pinnacle Forum

"Dee Duke's book, *Prayer Quest,* is the most powerful prayer tool I have encountered in 35
years of ministry. This book has been especially effective in changing the prayer lives of men,
and has mobilized them to becoming leaders of prayer in their families and in the church. Its
use in our small groups has heightened the process of meaningful prayer."

Dr. Richard L. Hagenbaugh
Senior Pastor, Gateway Baptist Church

"*Prayer Quest* inspired me to lead a more prayerful life and, as a result, a closer walk with
God. The study questions especially prompted me to approach both my business and my personal life with a more prayerful attitude. I highly recommend this book to anyone struggling
with his or her worship life."

Rick I. Johnson
President, De Minimis Inc. Environmental Management

"Most books I simply read and retire to a shelf. Dee Duke's work on prayer I reference . . . over
and over again. Why? Because it doesn't just tell me about prayer—it calls me to prayer in
ways that help even the most scattered soul (me) *practice* this more precious of all spiritual

disciplines. Life-changing riches are found in these pages. Don't miss them."

Bert Downs
President, Western Seminary

"If you believe prayer makes things happen, you have come to the right place. If you've been wondering about prayer and whether you should deepen this aspect of your life, this is a great spot for you too. Fresh truth lurks between these covers. There is no telling what may happen if you let it out."

Jay Carty
Author, *Coach Wooden, One on One*

"Reading *Prayer Quest* was, and continues to be, a life-changing experience. It has changed my whole approach to my business and personal life. Through this book, and through our church's prayer ministry, I have learned how to take my prayer life and turn it into a tool for accomplishing goals."

Gary Brown
CEO, G. Brown Enterprises, Inc.

"My personal discipline of prayer under the ministry of Pastor Dee has been the most extraordinary spiritual work of my life. Praying for my employees has intensified my commitment to do justice for them. Praying over important decisions gives confidence that my business practices are aligned with my values. As a business leader, I have found that a commitment to prayer also makes good business."

Jerry McIntosh, MBA, CHE
Chief Operations Officer, Samaritan Albany General Hospital

"I have observed that most movers and shakers who want to activate change claim they are too busy to pray. Dee is a mover and shaker, and has pioneered new ground teaching entrepreneurs how to pray their dreams and disappointments. This book has changed my spiritual and natural life."

John Bradley
President, IDAK Group, Inc.

PRAYER QUEST

BREAKING THROUGH TO YOUR
GOD-GIVEN DREAMS AND DESTINY

Dee Duke
with Brian Smith

NAVPRESS

Pray! Books • P.O. Box 35004 • Colorado Springs, CO 80935 • www.praymag.com

Pray! Books are published by NavPress. NavPress is the publishing ministry of The Navigators, an international Christian organization whose mission is to reach, disciple, and equip people to know Christ and to make Him known through successive generations.

Visit the *Pray!* website at www.praymag.com.

Printed in the Canada
1 2 3 4 5 6 7 8 9 10/09 08 07 06 05 04

(A version of this book was previously published under the title *The Time Is Now: Developing a Lifestyle of Prayer.*)

Contents

Foreword

Someone has said that "to know and not to do is not to know at all." When we are presented with a new book on a topic like prayer, we have the right, even the responsibility, to question whether the author is a practitioner—whether he is speaking from true and substantial experience. I can attest that God has indeed raised up a "knower" and a "doer" who lives what he teaches, and who knows how to lead churches toward becoming houses of prayer.

Dee Duke's church ministry has captured the attention of Christian leadership nationwide. Hundreds of people in his own church are significantly involved in ministries of prayer because of his direction and vision, and he has also conveyed this vision to hundreds of pastors. No one has counted how many additional hundreds of people in their churches have experienced revolution in prayer!

This book is a guide for any believer who wishes to rise to God's invitation and instruction regarding prayer. It also includes a special emphasis for equipping leaders to make prayer the basis of their ministry. I wholeheartedly recommend this long-awaited resource material.

—Dr. Joe Aldrich, former president,
Multnomah Bible College and Seminary,
Portland, Oregon

Preface

It has been my privilege to conduct my pilgrimage alongside Dee Duke over the past decade as a friend, ministry colleague, and co-leader on a leadership team for the Church of the Valley, a regional expression of the body of Christ in Oregon's mid-Willamette Valley. Both Dee and I were profoundly impacted and shaped by our exposure to the pastor's prayer summit movement, as well as trips to Argentina.

In twenty-five years of ministry, I've crossed paths with a lot of leaders. Not often enough have I seen their walk line up with their talk. There is something distinctive about Dee Duke. When he decided to put the principles of prayer into practice, he meant it, and he has done it. It is one thing to have a passion, another to preach it effectively. But it is a rare thing to find a man who builds a truth consistently into his daily life-showing it can be done—and then leads others to follow.

As the truest testimony to Dee's qualification to teach about prayer, I can point to Dee's wife and children, and to many in his congregation, who have learned to talk and walk with God. Dee has also earned the respect of the pastors and leaders of our valley.

As you seek the *delight* and *privilege* of personal prayer, as well as its discipline, you'll find yourself, more and more, abiding in the Vine, asking according to His Word and will, and bearing lasting fruit that glorifies the Father.

Join with me in imitating the example of a godly man, as he has consistently imitated Christ (Philippians 4:9; 1 Corinthians 11:1).

—Tom White, president, Frontline Ministries, Corvallis, Oregon

Introduction

My Story

Supernatural, miraculous living is all too rare. God says that normal life in Jesus is characterized by supernatural love in all our relationships, along with eager expectation of His mighty deeds accomplished in our lives. He calls us *now* to dream His dreams, to ask Him daily to display His power.

It took me more than a decade of ministry to learn this . . . and I'm still learning.

The study book you hold is part of the fruit God has borne through a wide variety of experiences, both good and bad, in the life of one man—a farm boy named Dee Duke . . . that's me. Because so much of what I will share through these lessons has grown out of my own experience, I invite you to start with an overview of my life. Then the specific life lessons I share later will make more sense, as you are able to place them in their context.

Marked from Birth

My story begins before I was born. My mom eloped with a sailor when she was fifteen and Dad was twenty-five. Mom had grown up attending church and living according to her family's principles, but all of that was abandoned when she and Dad married. A year later I was born, the first of five kids in the space of seven years.

We were stationed at a naval base in Kodiak, Alaska, when, at age six, I was critically injured by an earthmover at a construction site. My right leg was broken in six places, and I suffered additional life-threatening internal injuries. When my mom found me at the hospital, the doctor said, "Call your husband. Your son will not live much longer."

Dad was not to be found. Mom, in her helplessness, sought out the hospital chapel and there recommitted her life to the Lord. She emerged to better news. My life was no longer in danger, but my leg would have to be amputated.

So Mom returned to the chapel and made a deal with God. "Lord," she said, "If you save my son's leg, I'll be sure he's in church, Sunday school, whatever . . . every time the church doors are open." She came out again to learn that the doctors had managed to save my leg, but that I was bound to be crippled for life.

Again she bartered with God. "Lord, if you will fully heal my son, then I will devote him fully to you. I'll pray for him daily and commit him to your service." Now, she refrained from telling me the full extent of this story until after I had become a pastor, not wanting me to feel obligated to fulfill her commitment to God. God honored her request and restored me to full health and functioning. Mom kept her promise, too, faithfully praying every day for all five of us kids. Through these circumstances, God made prayer a key ingredient in my life, long before I became convinced of its importance. I was set up from the start.

Mom also kept her promise regarding church attendance. Sunday morning, Sunday night, Wednesday night and anything in between—we were there. On this she allowed no debate. If there were five vacation Bible schools at five churches in the area, I attended them all.

From Contentment to Frustration

Dad retired from twenty-two years of navy service when I was twelve. Dad had never tired of dreaming about that day when he would be free to buy a farm and live the life he had longed for. So I grew up with a farm mentality, even before we moved to our first purchase in Southern Oregon, and later to our dairy in Washington. I inherited my dad's passion for farming; it was all I wanted to do the rest of my life.

I married my wife Patty when I was twenty-one, content to share with her the life I had made for myself. In my mid-twenties, I attended two years of Bible college away from home for the sole purpose of preparing to help with the youth group at our home church. While away, my required student ministry happened to involve us in a brand new little church in Jefferson, Oregon. When I graduated in 1975, I returned to farming in Washington again.

Patty and I were disappointed to learn that we couldn't have children, and six years of childless marriage seemed to confirm this diagnosis. But then our daughter arrived—the first of eight kids! I was sure I had it all. What more could I possibly want from life?

My contentment was shattered when I was invited to become Jefferson Baptist Church's senior pastor. For six months I agonized. How could God be so wrong about me? I was afraid of pastoring. I didn't like people. Give me cows any day! Yet God brought me here in October 1976, and I've shepherded this flock for more than twenty-seven years.

Now, looking back, I see those years dividing cleanly into two seasons. For the first twelve years my lack of experience and people skills led to decidedly mixed results. I didn't love my people, and they knew it. Ongoing conflict within the church kept us from growing past a certain threshold. More than a decade of anxiety and pressure had so worn me down that I was convinced I had no choice but to leave the ministry. My decision to become a pastor had been a mistake all along.

Breakthrough to Fulfillment

In February 1989, God brought that first season of my ministry to an end and raised the curtain on a previously unimaginable adventure of fulfilled dreams and loving relationships in ministry.

Joe Aldrich, president of Multnomah School of the Bible, launched the first regional pastor's prayer summit at the Oregon coast. The letter describing the four-day, agenda-free, multi-denominational prayer event held absolutely no appeal to me, an agenda-bound, Conservative

Baptist. So I threw it away. Then came a second letter informing me that some rich guy had paid our way and that there would be free books. I started to think, *You know, this might be a nice vacation. I'll go, eat the meals, skip all the prayer sessions, have some nice walks on the beach, write my letter of resignation and come home . . . and get some free books in the process.*

God had other plans. It was during those four days that I "got saved" and devoted myself fully to prayer. It was there that I realized I had tried everything as a pastor except prayer. Books, seminars, programs . . . nothing provided me the keys to a thriving ministry. I even believed in prayer, but I had mistakenly assumed that traditional, convenient, comfortable prayer was all that was needed. It fit my schedule.

At one point during the prayer summit, Dr. Aldrich explained that his best prayer times came when he prayed for an hour or more at a sitting. That sparked a question in my mind. *Have I, at any time in my life, ever spent an hour alone in uninterrupted prayer?* I couldn't think of a single instance in all my forty years. I then began to understand how I had been spiritually starving myself, my ministry, and the people around me. I suddenly knew why so much of my ministry and personal experience had been negative. I had been praying just enough to convince myself I was satisfying God—a practice I call "token prayer"—but not nearly enough to call myself a man of prayer. I committed simply to pray more. The missing ingredient in my unhappy ministry career had been the *quantity* of time talking to God—*sheer volume of prayer.*

Years earlier, even before I finished high school, I had learned that new commitments don't keep themselves. Summer after summer I would return from church camp, passionately excited about a new commitment. Six weeks later the commitment was gone, forgotten. After several of these disappointing experiences, I approached my pastor. His counsel has guided me ever since. First, he said, I needed to make my commitments specific. Second, I needed to write them down. And third, I needed to read them regularly. I followed his advice as a junior in high school, and, for the first time, I made a commitment that lasted longer than six weeks. In fact, it became an integral part of my life.

So, years later, on the bus ride back from the prayer summit, I took out a yellow legal pad and wrote a list of seven specific goals, topped by my commitment to become a man devoted to prayer. Twelve years of frustration and anxiety were enough for me. I determined to readjust my priorities. I read those goals every day after I returned, and my commitments to prayer and love took solid root in my life and in my church. The fifteen years since that day have demonstrated to me, beyond any doubt, that faithful prayer must lie at the foundation of any fulfilling life or thriving ministry. And God has shown me that love is a commitment, not just an emotion, and that prayer is the most effective demonstration of love toward God and people. These have been the most effective and fulfilling years of my personal and ministry life.

What Does God Have in Store for You?

As you progress through this study, I invite you to consider God's promises and commands related to prayer. His Word tells us clearly that the praying man, woman, or church will impact the world in ways that can't be explained naturally—only supernaturally. And my own experience underscores the fact that faithful prayer will surely lead to supernatural life and love. Take a chance on the possibility that God really means what He says. Give it some time. Then watch what the God of all creation will do . . . because you pray.

How to Use This Book

Welcome to the reality where dreams come true! God has a dream, and it is certain to happen just as He imagines it. He has placed the stamp of His image on our souls, so that we also dream great dreams. As we learn to passionately share and enjoy God's dreams, we will see Him work in amazing ways, accomplishing great things through our ordinary lives.

You can begin *now* on the path toward this life of fulfilled passions. This book is intended to help you learn to walk so intimately with God that you will see Him fulfill His dreams in and through you. Toward this end, we've designed this study with several important features.

Flexibility

This study guide is designed to meet the needs of a variety of groups and individuals. The first seven lessons contain biblical principles that clearly pertain to everyone who wants to grow in his or her prayer life. Lessons 8-12 also have value for every reader, but because they cover more specialized topics, you are encouraged to select which of these will be most profitable in your group or individual study.

Each lesson may be completed in a single sitting, or you may wish to complete a page or two each day, spreading the study over several days each week.

Each lesson includes an optional section at the end entitled "Going Further and Deeper," providing additional scriptural study and practical insight. You can complete this portion during the same week as the rest of the lesson, or you may choose to return to it at a later time.

Relevance for Real Life

As you deal with the teaching portions and Scripture study questions, think of this as more than merely a cognitive exercise. You will regularly encounter instructions for putting each lesson's principles into practice in your daily life. You will gain the most from this study if you take these opportunities seriously, making time to do the suggested exercises, in order to learn the principles of healthy, biblical prayer through actual experience.

Each lesson ends with a suggested Scripture passage for meditation and memorization. You are encouraged to simply write this passage out on a card and carry it around with you through the week. As you read the passage over and over, considering and praying over its meaning and implications in your life, in a matter of time (shorter than you might think) you'll probably find that you have the words memorized.

The Value of Encouragement

Experience has shown that you will learn and apply the principles of Scripture much more effectively if you face the same growth challenges alongside others. *This point cannot be stressed enough.* If you are not already planning to work through this study as part of a study group or a partnership, please seriously consider finding at least one other person who will complete the first seven lessons, or more, with you. Even if you simply meet periodically to share new thoughts and new steps you're taking, you will be able to encourage each other to put God's Word into action in your lives. For practical principles that will help you create a safe, growth-producing environment in your group or partnership, see Lesson 10, "Accountability that Works."

Respect for Each Person's God-Given Design

Finally, keep in mind that, while prayer is a discipline God wishes everyone to cultivate, some of the specific techniques proposed in this book will work for some people better than for others. Along the way, you will find suggested alternatives that may fit your personal preferences and schedule better than others. Lesson 5, "Gifting and Approaches to Prayer," will help you understand these differences and how to make the most of your unique qualities in your prayer life.

Prayer Troubleshooting Guide

Please refer back to this page at any time throughout your study, in order to address needs as they may arise.

▸ Do you feel overwhelmed by the discipline of prayer?

　🔆Read Appendix B, "Help! I'm Drowning!" on page 155.

▸ Do you feel apathetic, lacking motivation to pray?

　🔆Read Appendix C, "Help! I'm Stuck!" on page 159.

▸ Do you feel as though you've given up on dreams you had when your faith was new?

　🔆Begin with Lesson 1, "Daring to Dream Again" on page 21.

▸ Do you feel your prayer preferences are inferior or superior to those of others?

　🔆Look ahead to Lesson 5, "Gifting and Approaches to Prayer" on page 61.

▸ Do you find yourself at a loss as to what to pray?

　🔆Look ahead to Lesson 6, "What to Pray for People" on page 71.

▸ Are you becoming aware that you can't grow in the discipline of prayer by yourself?

　🔆Look ahead to Lesson 10, "Accountability that Works" on page 113.

▸ Do you feel directionless, wanting to grow but unsure how to proceed?

　🔆Look ahead to Lesson 11, "Growth through Goals" on page 123.

▸ Are you a family, ministry, or church leader who wants those under your care to grow in prayer?

　🔆Focus attention on Lesson 7 and Lesson 12 on pages 81 and 133.

Part 1

CENTRAL ISSUES

DARING TO DREAM AGAIN

~⊚~

"Now to him who is able to do immeasurably more than all we ask or imagine, according to his power that is at work within us, to him be glory in the church and in Christ Jesus throughout all generations for ever and ever! Amen."

—Ephesians 3:20-21

"Open your eyes and the whole world is full of God."

—Jakob Böhme, German mystic (1575-1624)

Longings Long Denied

Imagine that I have had nothing to eat or drink for three full days. At the end of the three days, you ask me, "How are you doing?" And I answer, "I'm just fine. No problem."

I continue my fast until I've been totally without food or drink for ten days, and you ask me, "How are you now?" I answer, "No problem. I'm not hungry or thirsty. I'm great."

If this persisted for two or three weeks, I'd probably end up dead. But, assuming I survived, what would you conclude about me? You'd know I was deeply into denial.

There is another kind of hunger we suppress. Every human individual has been designed to achieve greatness. Each of us has been created in the image and likeness of God. Every believer has been purchased by the sacrifice of Christ, and the Almighty Holy Spirit lives in each of us. Because of these incredible truths, there is deep within every person a longing for significance, a passion to accomplish something great, along with everything we need in order to do it! When we suppress that longing, we deny a driving life force.

Most believers watch the few outstanding dreamers and achievers, and we continue through our average lives, saying, "That's okay. God hasn't gifted me. I'm too timid. I'm not strong. I'll just finish out my remaining years trying to be good, and that will be fine." Yet deep down inside, there's a voice screaming, "No! It's not fine! I want to accomplish something great!" It's a voice many of us haven't paid any attention to in years.

It's time to wake up! It's time to listen to our God-given longings for significance. It's time to kindle the flame of passion that smolders inside each of us. The Almighty eagerly awaits the rebirth of your zeal, that He might accomplish great things through you. Now is the time to dream!

The Dream Promised

Two thousand years ago, on the darkest night of history, the Messiah spoke to His men, knowing His execution had, for eternity past, been scheduled for the following day. Three years of miraculous deeds and authoritative teaching were coming to a paradoxical close. The Son of God, who had raised the dead, now spoke of His own imminent passage through the cold portal of death. Bewildered fear filled their hearts.

The disciples heard Jesus begin, "I tell you the truth," words He had often used to grab His hearers' attention for an especially significant revelation. To a man, the disciples gathered their distracted thoughts and focused their senses on the Teacher:

> "I tell you the truth, anyone who has faith in me will do what I have been doing. He will do even greater things than these, because I am going to the Father" (John 14:12).

1. If you have placed faith in Christ, then this promise is yours! Take a moment and jot down a few works you know Jesus did during His life on earth.

2. Now consider Jesus' amazing promise to you. In your wildest dreams and fantasies, perhaps from the early days after you first trusted Christ, what is the greatest quest you've ever dreamed of pursuing? (List more than one if you wish.)

3. Are you still pursuing your quest? If not, why do you think you abandoned it?

The Dream Abandoned

The most common reason that most believers have given up dreaming God's dreams is illustrated by Jesus in Matthew 25:14-30.

4. Read this parable, paying close attention to the third servant. This man had somehow learned that risks—even those required in order to obey his master—were too dangerous. In what ways have your dreams been squashed by disappointment and caution in the past?

5. Whenever you or someone else voices a dream that seems impractical, what thoughts go through your mind?

Rekindling the Dream

6. Now reread Matthew 25:14-30, focusing on the first two servants (notice "went at once" in v. 16). What was the attitude of these men toward the risks of pursuing a dream?

7. What might the Lord bring about in your life as you prove faithful to imagine and pursue His dreams (vv. 19-23, 29)?

8. Isaiah 42:13 and 59:17 describe the way in which God goes about His business. We are made in His image and likeness (Genesis 1:26-27). What, then, do these Isaiah passages reveal about our potential for pursuing a dream?

zealously stirred up

Quite often God's dreams, and ours, take the form of concrete, specific plans, otherwise known as goals or commitments. Some of us feel confined by the idea of a goal or commitment and would prefer to stay "free" for God's spontaneous leading. But Scripture clearly shows that God often reveals His dreams and plans hours, years, and even centuries in advance, and that pursuit of these dreams can be even more exciting than living spontaneously. We'll examine this aspect of God's way of operating in Lesson 10, "Growth through Goals."

9. What do these passages teach about God's dream for each of us?

Titus 2:14

purify us for Himself, to be His own special people, zealous for good works

Romans 12:10-12

filled with brotherly love, kindly affectionate

Joshua 1:7-8

prospering in what we do, successful

It's often said you pay a price for success, but that's not true. You pay a price for failure due to apathy. That price is misery.

> *If you would prosper in your work, be sure to keep up earnest desires and expectations of success. If your hearts be not set on the end of your labors, and you long not to see the conversion and edification of your hearers, and do not study and preach in hope, you are not likely to see much suc-*

cess. As it is a sign of a false, self-seeking heart, that can be content to be still doing, and yet see no fruit of his labor; so I have observed that God seldom blesseth any man's work so much as his, whose heart is set upon the success of it.

—Richard Baxter, *The Reformed Pastor*

You may be one who, for years, has put on a happy face, living out an adequate life, just like others you know. You are satisfied with a house, a car, a lawn, and a dog. But the pleasant facade does nothing to change what you feel inside—fear, despair, inadequacy, low self-worth.

Pay attention to the hunger God has placed in you, and you will do yourself the greatest favor ever. When God stirs your imagination with a dream, challenge your fear. Step up and say, "I love You, Lord. Here I am. Send me." Not a single person was ever designed for mediocrity. Every one was designed for greatness.

A dream is a desire felt so strongly that we think and meditate on it constantly until we see it in our mind as clearly as if it were reality. A dream believes that what is desired will happen; it is accompanied by anticipation and positive expectation. People who dream tend to be upbeat and enthusiastic. They give hope to those around them, attracting people to their dreams and causes.

10. According to 2 Timothy 1:6-7, Psalm 37:4, and Haggai 1:14, what is our part and what is God's part in stirring our passion?

Our part	God's part
stir up our gifts	giving the Spirit / power, / love, / a sound / mind
delight in the Lord	giving us our desires
to come and work	to stir up our spirits

Prayer and Dreams

Let's return once more to that darkest of all nights, the eve of the Messiah's execution. In the face of apparent defeat, Jesus proclaimed His eternal sovereignty and victory.

11. Read John 14:12-14. Immediately on the heels of His promise to do even greater works through us, how does Jesus explain the means by which He will accomplish these things (vv. 13-14)?

12. Prayer—risky, passionate prayer—is the tool God will use to fulfill great dreams through you and me. List a few words and phrases that describe the kind of prayer habit you would like to develop, in order to become God's instrument to accomplish the miraculous.

Charles Spurgeon sang a lot. Someone once asked him, "Why do you sing so much?" He answered, "Because I'm happy." This begged the next question, "Why are you so happy?" His answer: "Because I sing."

In the same way, prayer and passion have a reciprocal effect. If you begin to pray more, your passion for God's dreams increases. As your passion grows, you long to pray more that God will do great things through you. God will use those who want to be used greatly. Acknowledge your built-in sense of destiny, your hunger for significance. Fan that spark, seek God's heart, and soon you'll shine with a white hot flame, and the miraculous will flow out of your life.

13. Read Psalms 86:3 and 88:1. Why would anyone pray all day or night?

Through the lessons to follow, you'll make several key decisions about the particulars of your prayer life. At this point, take a few minutes to talk to your Father, who has granted you the privilege of prayer. Tell Him your dreams for your future, and enjoy His pleasure.

The Next Step

At the end of each lesson, you'll be prompted to put your commitment to prayer into practice. Glance ahead at Appendix A: "Twenty Steps to Daily Prayer," beginning on page 147, and choose your personal starting point. Take it easy; better to enjoy a little prayer at first than to frustrate yourself. If "Going Further and Deeper" below is an exercise you could realistically do at least once a week, while including a few minutes of prayer each of the other days, then you might start with Step 9 or 10.

Memory Passage

"I tell you the truth, anyone who has faith in me will do what I have been doing. He will do even greater things than these, because I am going to the Father."

—John 14:12

Going Further and Deeper

Dream Notes

This exercise is one of many ways to release your imagination to the Lord in prayer, and to seek His heart and mind in an attitude of worship. Consider using it at least once a week, as part of your new journey. Developing a new habit requires focus and determination. If this exercise doesn't appeal to you, please adapt it or choose an alternative (see "Twenty Steps to Daily Prayer," page 147). Feel free to seek your own best prayer pattern as you continue through these studies.

1. Envision yourself embarking on a day trip into the presence of God. Travel as light as possible, leaving behind the pressing issues of life. Envision yourself approaching God in His glory. Read and meditate on Revelation 4:1-4. Stand in awe of the grandeur of God. Revel in the privilege of His presence. Read Psalm 145, preferably aloud.

2. Acknowledge to your Father your desire to offer praise to Him and to dream with Him about His best for you and your life.

3. Ask God to bring to mind any sinful attitudes, words or actions, or any unresolved conflicts that hinder your relationship with Him. Read Psalm 139:13-16, 23-24. As you think of anything needing attention, confess it to God—that is, simply agree with Him about it. Thank God that you are forgiven through the blood of Jesus.

4. Read Psalm 150, preferably aloud.

5. Ask your Father to lift you up to His chart room where He keeps the blueprints of His dreams and plans. Ask Him to open your heart to His desires for you (Psalm 37:4). Throughout the rest of your prayer session, especially during times of silence, write down any thoughts that cross your mind, numbering each thought on a separate line (you will refer back to these at another time). Do not judge or be critical of your thoughts now—just let them flow.

6. Go back and continue to read selected passages from Psalms 145-150 (Also see Psalms 8, 19, 33, and 104). Keep asking God to make clear His desires for you, and continue writing down your thoughts. *during all scripture reading*

7. When your allotted dream time with God has ended, fold your notes and put them in your Bible or prayer journal. Determine to dream with God again within a week (write it into your schedule as an appointment). At that next meeting, repeat steps 1-6, leaving an additional ten or fifteen minutes free.

8. Take out and review your previous list of dream notes. Circle those dream notes you wish to pursue further. Pray about these circled thoughts: *Father, please help me to understand whether this thought is from You or from some other source. Help me to discern which thoughts are worthy of Your dream for my life.*

Your dream notes may stem from one of four sources (although discerning between these is difficult and not always necessary):

- Thoughts from God.
- Your own original thoughts.
- Thoughts from the world (good, neutral, or evil sources).
- Thoughts from Satan and his demons.

Careful prayer, reflection, and review, especially based on your current knowledge of God's Word, can help you isolate the dream notes you are confident are guided and provided by God.

9. Select the dream notes you believe God wishes you to pursue, and translate them into goal statements: "I plan to. . . ." Give each goal a starting date. Begin with small goals. Be careful about major goals that are new to you. If they are truly from God, He will persist in bringing them to your mind over time.

10. Continue practicing your dreaming with God. The Good Shepherd says that His sheep recognize His voice (John 10:1-5). As you grow in your familiarity with Him, you can expect to become better at recognizing His desires for each day, week, month, and year of your life . . . and even His lifetime plans for you will become clearer.

11. *Caution:* Should you experience a strong leading or prompting through these prayer times that requires a major change in your life—a large expenditure, extended commitment, or change of relationship—move carefully. God is not forgetful, and you won't miss anything of true importance if you act with prudence. For major decisions, please seek advice from at least three people of prayer you respect before taking action.

THE BLESSINGS OF PRAYER

~⃝~

"I know no blessing so small as to be reasonably expected without prayer,

nor any so great but may be attained by it."

—Robert South, English clergyman (1634-1716)

"Ask and it will be given to you; seek and you will find; knock and the door

will be opened to you. For everyone who asks receives; he who seeks finds; and

to him who knocks, the door will be opened. . . . If you then, though you are

evil, know how to give good gifts to your children, how much more will your

Father in heaven give the Holy Spirit to those who ask him!"

—Luke 11:9-13

" the Spirit of power, of love and a sound mind "

II Tim 1: 6, 7

A Bowlful of Blessing

There is in my life a particular discipline, and I have yet to find anyone who can claim to be my equal at maintaining it. In fact, I haven't found anyone who even comes close to my commitment. It is the discipline of eating a bowl of ice cream every night.

What? You're surprised that I would call eating ice cream a discipline? But why can't something that brings me great pleasure be a discipline? Or, conversely, why can't a discipline bring me great pleasure?

Prayer is better than ice cream! In my life, disciplined prayer results in joyous blessing in my marriage, my family, my church, and my community. Why? Because prayer says, "I love You," to God, and is the greatest expression of love toward people. Yes, prayer can be hard work, but why avoid a practice that guarantees some of the greatest rewards in all the universe?

The Critical Ingredient

If I were to choose one way to make my prayer more effective, and so to bring into my life more of God's blessing, what might that be? I've come to the firm conclusion that the most important ingredient missing in most of our prayer lives today is simply volume . . . quantity. The more I pray, the more God blesses me and those around me.

In 2 Corinthians 9:6, Paul explains the law of the harvest:

"Remember this: whoever sows sparingly will also reap sparingly, and whoever sows generously will also reap generously."

The context of this verse has to do with giving, but the principle is applicable to all spiritual investments, including the investment of prayer. This is why our church motto has become:

"Much prayer, much blessing.
Little prayer, little blessing.
No prayer, no blessing."

There are certainly other factors besides quantity that affect the "horsepower" of one's prayer life, such as my attitude of love in prayer, and the character issues in 1 Peter 3:7 and Psalm 66:18. But, given two believers whose character qualities are otherwise the same, I maintain that the person who prays more will enjoy more blessing.

How much should you pray? That depends. How much do you want to be blessed? If you

ask for

want an abundance of blessings like love, joy, peace, and patience, deeper relational fulfillment with others, or the salvation of believing friends and loved ones, then pray a lot! Once I
came to a full awareness of this principle, I began to squeeze as much prayer as possible into
each day. And, indeed, God has blessed me, my family, and my church accordingly. I know
from experience—it works!

What kinds of blessings am I talking about? Let's look at a few that come directly from the
promises of God's Word.

Seven Blessings of Prayer

**A. Prayer expresses supernatural love for God, each other, and the world—
and results in more love.** When most people say, "I love you," they mean, "You make
me happy." But biblical love, produced through prayer, goes even further to say, "I'm committed to you, no matter what you do."

When we receive God's love in prayer, and when we tell God repeatedly "I love You" by
praying, we also begin to appropriate supernatural love for others. Especially those people
who seem to rub us the wrong way. I learned that as I prayed repeatedly by name for people I
didn't relate to, it became easier to talk to them and to care about them. As a result, they said
they felt more loved. When we pray for people, God intervenes in relationships and makes up
for some of our mistakes.

*1. What do Paul's prayer requests tell you about the love God will provide as you pray
for people?*

Philippians 1:9

"*abounding*" *love has to have channels
as it overflows*

1 Thessalonians 3:12

2. Why is Jesus' "new commandment" impossible to fulfill without prayer (John 13:34-35)?

B. Prayer builds relational unity. Believers are more likely to take steps of obedience in the safe environment of unity—a unity that must be maintained by the supernatural presence of God. God's people will experience spiritual growth and energizing joy, and
unbelievers will see the supernatural in our lives—all to God's glory.

3. Unity topped Jesus' prayer request list (John 17:11, 20-21). How would greater unity in your relationships be a blessing to you?

Notice that Jesus made unity within the Trinity the standard for believers as well. How can people ever become as unified as the Godhead? Only through prayer and God's resultant blessing.

4. Now turn to Acts 2:42-47 and 4:32. Notice in 2:42 the devotion to prayer. Describe this community in your own words.

C. Prayer deepens your relationship with God, enhancing the power of His presence in your life. When I was twelve, my Uncle Bill, whom I had never met, visited my family. One day early in his visit, he beckoned me and handed me a nickel. Being a well-mannered young man, I thanked him and moved on. A little later, he handed me another nickel. I then noticed that his pocket was full of the coins. In 1960, a nickel was worth much more than it is today, especially to a twelve-year-old boy! Soon I worked up the courage to ask my uncle for a nickel. My mother was on me in an instant. But Uncle Bill interrupted her lecture about manners. He pulled me over and said, "Dee, you ask me for a nickel any time you want."

So I did! At first I politely spaced my requests out over reasonable intervals, which became shorter as my cash account increased. I took sudden interest in everything Uncle Bill did. Where he sat, I sat. When he watched TV, I watched. When he went for a walk, I went too.

A couple days later, I worked up the nerve to say, "Uncle Bill, I have an idea. This is going to save you a lot of time. How about just giving me all your nickels now, so I won't have to keep bothering you?"

But Uncle Bill said, "You know, one reason I came was to spend time with you kids. Now, I know how boys are. You don't have time for your old Uncle Bill, so I came up with this plan to bribe you into spending time with me. If I gave you all the nickels now, I wouldn't see you again. I'll keep the nickels. You keep asking as often as you want, and I'll keep giving them to you."

I got a lot of nickels during that visit. I also gained a valuable relationship with an uncle that I would never otherwise have known as well.

Similarly, God calls us to frequent, increasingly intimate conversation, so that He might pour out more blessing into our lives. Now, if I were God, I would have designed a more practical plan, such as the "Santa Claus approach," where we dump all the requests once a year. But without frequent investment of time, we would forget God, and our relationship with Him would never grow. He values our company far more than we value His. And so He has tied prayer to blessing in order that we might come to Him often, to lead us eventually to treasure the greatest blessing of all—Himself and His presence with us.

5. According to each of the following passages, why is a deeper relationship with God a blessing to you?

Psalm 27:4-14

Psalm 73:25-28

D. Prayer produces the fruit of a positive attitude—joy, confidence, security, faith, and peace. When we fill our lives with prayer, the whining drops off, and existence becomes considerably more enjoyable. We recognize the good in our circumstances, in others and in God, coming closer to perpetual joy and gratitude (Philippians 4:4; 1 Thessalonians 5:16-18). We become attractive and edifying to others. The problems don't all go away, but if you pray about them daily (Philippians 4:6-7), they fade in comparison to all there is to be grateful and joyful for.

6. How would your typical, daily patterns of thought be different if the truths of these passages were deeply integrated into your heart?

Psalm 16:11

Ephesians 1:18-23

Philippians 4:6-7

E. Prayer produces spiritual growth. It is thoroughly appropriate to pray for your own character growth and maturity. Even as you pray about other matters, time in His presence changes you to be more like Him.

7. What if you regularly prayed the prayer of Ephesians 3:14-19 for yourself? What changes would you see as God began to answer?

F. Prayer produces boldness, courage, and passion to reach lost friends, neighbors, and relatives for Christ. Prayer cultivates inside you the heart of Jesus—compassion for people in need. At first, you might pray for lost people simply because it's the right thing to do. But as you persist, you will gain Christ's heart, the heart that caused Him to come to earth, to suffer and to die.

8. Why was it necessary for even the zealous apostle Paul to depend on prayer for his passion in witnessing (Ephesians 6:19)?

G. Prayer combats Satan's influence over you and others. Our enemy is skillful and powerful. He wants nothing more than to destroy us and our impact on the world. It's hard enough to fight something you can see, but you can't smash a fist or drive a sword into this enemy (unless of course it is the Sword of the Spirit, the Word of God). However, you can call on God Almighty, and He will fight the battle for you. Especially if you have any role of leadership—even as a parent—your God-given authority to impact other lives through prayer surpasses privilege. It's a sobering responsibility.

9. What do you learn about prayer and spiritual warfare from each of the following?

John 17:15

2 Corinthians 4:4

2 Corinthians 11:3

Ephesians 6:12,18

Read Exodus 17:9-13. There were two wars being fought here—one visible, one invisible. The winner of the invisible war determined the winner of the visible war. Moses' uplifted hands represented intercession on behalf of God's people. We must fight the same way. We can win the war, first in the invisible realm, then in the visible.

Now read Jesus' words in Luke 22:31-32. When we pray faithfully, God responds to faith and strengthens us to stand against anything. We can then walk in confidence and security under God's protection.

10. In light of the preceding two passages, name two or three people you can pray for, and describe the ways in which your prayers might result in their protection.

11. Take a few minutes now to tell God what blessings you desire most from Him. Don't worry. That's not selfish. He wants to bless you! Look back through this lesson for ideas.

12. Now spend several more minutes talking to Him about the investment you are considering making, in order to receive His blessings and to know Him better. You may still be tentative, not quite ready for a firm, specific commitment. Take your time deciding. Write below some of your ideas about the commitment you might make.

The Next Step

Turn now to "Twenty Steps to Daily Prayer" (page 147) and continue reaping the benefits by taking the next step this week.

Memory Passage

"Remember this: whoever sows sparingly will also reap sparingly, and whoever sows generously will also reap generously."

—2 Corinthians 9:6

Going Further and Deeper

This lesson by no means presents an exhaustive list of the blessings of prayer, but we've seen some of the most important. Here are a few more, drawn from Scripture and my experience.

Prayer produces heart desire to do the work of the ministry. At our church, we start new ministries, not in response to needs, but in response to expressed desires by those who want to do ministry. God has given many of our people hunger for impact, and our church is thriving with ministry. I can't keep track of all that's going on! Why? Because our church is a praying church. We call ourselves the "I love you" church. There's nothing like prayer to fill people with desire to serve, as God works in their hearts.

13. Summarize Ephesians 4:16 in your own words. What does the building of Christ's body, the church, require?

14. What might God do in your heart and the hearts of others if you were to follow regularly Jesus' instruction in Matthew 9:37-38?

Prayer results in opportunities to serve Christ and to advance the kingdom of God. We were all born for extraordinary accomplishment, and that is not a fleshly fantasy, but a dream rooted in God's purpose. Each of us naturally aspires to greatness. We long to do the truly significant, the unbelievable, the indescribable. But by adulthood, most of us have buried these dreams because of fear of failure, negative past experience, lack of hope, and our sense of insignificance.

Every believer is capable of being a champion for God, and a church full of such people can change the world. Yet, we're often unwilling to pay the price. What would happen if you and a group of fellow believers all prayerfully aspired to greatness? Prayer stimulates our dreams, along with the faith in God's ability to fulfill them, removing the mental obstacles. Start with faithfulness in the small responsibilities God sends your way, and, in time, He will use you to accomplish the great things through prayer.

15. Read Colossians 4:2-3, Acts 14:27, and Revelation 3:7-8. What are your dreams— perhaps forgotten dreams? What might the God of all the universe do through you when you commit yourself to faithful prayer?

The intimate conversation of prayer:

- **strengthens marriages and families,** especially if you pray together faithfully. Try also to think of your marriage and family as a model to impact others for eternity.

- **increases receptiveness to and understanding of God's voice.** Through prayer—a two-way conversation with God—we speak, and we learn to hear Him speak. Participation in prayer naturally enhances the quality of hearing God. It especially enhances our ability to understand God's Word, the Bible. It is always a good practice to keep a Bible open as you pray. *Read it and write down prayers*

- **improves vision.** All vision is from God. Vision is discernment of His will some distance into the future—the discernment of a plan for life, family, ministry. When I'm convinced that I've received vision from God, then I can move ahead with passion. I sometimes gain vision through prolonged prayer.

- **builds emotional strength and endurance in the face of trials.** The limit of your impact is your ability to manage pressure. And you can only manage pressure with the strength of God.

- **brings God's provision of wisdom for life decisions.** The more we pray, the more the Holy Spirit will minister to us. Acts 13:2-3 demonstrates this fact. The believers at Antioch were simply praying, worshiping, and fasting. There is no indication that they were seeking God for direction, but it clearly came. The Holy Spirit spoke, and the history of Christianity was forever changed.

Were they fasting for some clear directions?

LOVE—
THE REASON
WHY WE PRAY

∽◈∾

"Dear friends, let us love one another, for love comes from God. Everyone who loves has been born of God and knows God."

—1 John 4:7

"And now these three remain: faith, hope and love.
But the greatest of these is love."

—1 Corinthians 13:13

"Love" Is Spelled T-I-M-E

Starting into a new ministry position was extremely demanding. During my early years as pastor of Jefferson Baptist Church (JBC), the requirements of ministry, keeping up with the house, and providing for a growing family left me little time to spend with my wife, Patty. She would regularly ask me for time together, and I repeatedly disappointed her.

Finally her requests started to get on my nerves. In an effort to appease her, I came up with the perfect plan. I sat her down and said, "Honey, my one break during the week is Monday nights, watching football. How about if you sit and watch the games with me? Then we can talk during the commercials. Okay?"

It was most definitely *not* okay.

Patty knew something I didn't. She knew that she needed more than my leftovers. She needed me to treat her as one of the most important parts of my life and to spend substantial amounts of costly, precious time with her . . . undistracted, one-on-one time. I needed it, too, though I was slow to realize it.

It's the same in my connection with God. That also is a personal relationship, and it takes time—lots of it—in order to develop trust and love, that I might grow to know His heart. We all have a God-given need to make Him the most important priority in our lives.

The way we tell God He is important is by giving Him time *off the top* of our schedules, not from the leftovers. When we pray—and pray much—we are telling God, "I love You, and I want to know Your heart," and we open the door for Him to pour out the abundance of blessings He wants us to have.

Prayer and Loving People

Prayer is an expression of love to God. It's also an expression of love toward people.

This was never more vividly demonstrated than when I first devoted my life to prayer. After thirteen years as pastor of JBC, I had come to consider my ministry a total failure. The church had split several times, there was constant disunity, and people repeatedly told me they didn't feel I loved them.

I had tried every fix I could find—seminars, books, programs—everything except prayer. It was only when I started asking God to do what I was obviously unable to do myself that He took over and things began to change. I started praying three cumulative hours per day, praying with my wife, inviting people to pray with me at the church every morning and evening, and teaching my congregation about prayer.

That's when God unleashed a new dimension of His blessing.

I started feeling and acting differently toward people who had previously irritated me. They perceived that loving attitude toward them. Unity grew quickly throughout the church family. And we made such an impact within our community that, after only two months of our new prayer commitment, our congregation of eighty-one adults drew an Easter crowd of four hundred, and one hundred people prayed to receive Christ.

We became instant believers in the power of prayer to change our hearts and to change others around us. We learned that praying was the most loving thing we could do for people.

We also came to realize that we had never before really known God. My personal priorities and the priorities of the church quickly changed as we began to connect with Him, heart to heart. As a result, today we are the strongest single influence in the town of Jefferson. Neighbors regularly stop us to give us their prayer requests, because they know we love them and are devoted to them.

And the effects of prayerful love have spread around the world. In Sierra Leone, West Africa, we have established two schools, with about five hundred students each, and seven churches, with a cumulative attendance of more than two thousand members. We eagerly await the next miracle God will perform because we care and we pray.

1. According to each of these passages, how important is love in your relationships with God and with other people?

Matthew 22:37-40

Romans 13:8-10

1 Corinthians 16:14

Proverbs 15:17

When we are giving and receiving love, we are incredibly happy. When we aren't, we are incredibly miserable. Love is the basis of our sense of worth. It's as essential to our souls as breathing is to our physical bodies.

Only One Source
So, then, how do we go about giving and receiving love? First and foremost, by knowing we are loved by God.

When I was a freshman in college, some friends and I ministered weekly at a local mission, addressing the spiritual and physical needs of the homeless in downtown Portland. One of my friends took compassion on the homeless people as winter set in, and he came up with a plan to distribute gloves to as many as possible. He made arrangements with an army surplus store for a shipment of one hundred pairs of gloves. To make things even better, the store decided to donate the gloves.

Since we knew the news would cheer up the people coming to the mission, we announced ahead of time that the gloves were on their way. We would distribute them the week before Christmas.

The day came to pick up the shipment. But when my friend went to the store, the manager said, "I'm very sorry, but the shipment didn't arrive. It's not going to work out after all."

We were stunned. What would we tell all those hopeful people?

We hastily pooled our own money and managed to buy a disparaging twelve pairs of gloves. Compared to the crowd that showed up on the appointed night, our dozen gifts seemed like almost nothing. We passed them out and apologized profusely for the disappointment.

That evening I found myself speaking with one of the older men who had come—an outspoken codger for whom I had become quite fond. I apologized to him again, but he stopped me in mid-sentence: "Hey, no problem." Then he made one of the wisest statements I've ever heard. "You can't give away what you don't got."

The same is true with love. You can't give it if you haven't received God's love for you. And the more fully you comprehend God's love for you, the more you'll be free to give and receive love in your relationships with people.

Love is like a special kind of energy that you can only get from God. But in order to engage in loving relationships with people, you must *comprehend* God's love with your mind and heart. God's love is infinite, and our capacity to receive and give His love is infinite. But if we don't accept and experience the love of God, then it will make little impact in our lives.

I once heard about a village in China that depended on coal in the winter. One year the shipment of coal failed to arrive, and two-thirds of the people died. When the survivors started burying the bodies, they discovered great reserves of coal just two feet under the surface. The resources to save the village had been available all along, but because the people had not known about them, they did not benefit from them.

2. How does John describe the relationship between our love for others and God's love for us?

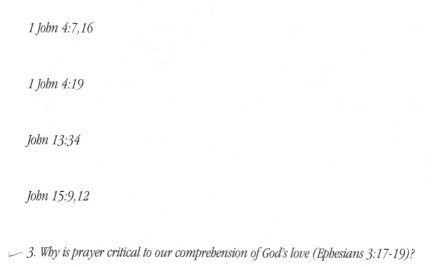

1 John 4:7,16

1 John 4:19

John 13:34

John 15:9,12

3. *Why is prayer critical to our comprehension of God's love (Ephesians 3:17-19)?*

4. *Why is prayer critical to our ability to give and receive love in our human relationships (1 Thessalonians 3:12-13)?*

How to Know God's Love

To the degree that we understand and accept God's love for us, to that degree we will be able to give it and receive it. So, then, how can we comprehend God's love?

I've discovered several ways in the Bible, but I want to focus here on the most important. The foremost way to comprehend God's love *is for Him to tell us that He loves us.*

5. *Describe in your own words the way that God communicates love to us, according to Romans 8:15-16.*

Some of us hear and receive God's loving affirmations more than others. Why is that?

It's because of the next principle, which is the central key to this entire lesson: *God communicates His love to our spirits when we verbally tell Him that we love Him.*

"Worship" is another word for telling God, "I love you." The more you tell Him that you love Him, the more He tells you the same in return. The extent of His love doesn't change, but your ability to comprehend and receive His love does.

6. How does James 4:8 apply to the expression and experience of love between us and God?

7. Read John 21:15-17. Jesus wasn't satisfied with Peter's assertion, "You know that I love you." What was Jesus waiting to hear? Why?

8. Why is the verbal expression of love so important (Proverbs 27:5)?

"I love you" was one of King David's favorite expressions to God (Psalm 18:1). Just as a car goes faster when you press on the gas, so also there is a direct relationship between our expression of love to God and His expression of love to us. I believe this is yet another application of the law of the harvest (Galatians 6:7; 2 Corinthians 9:6), which contends the more generously you sow, the more abundantly you will reap.

As we take this simple, but often difficult, step of verbalizing love to God and others, He places supernatural, overflowing love in our hearts so that we can love more. When we tell God, "I love you," and mean it as best we know how, we are holding up our pitcher, and He fills it to the brim, over and over and over. When you know without any doubt that you're loved by God, all the insecurities and fears that keep you from loving others fade away.

I encourage you to begin and end every prayer with "I love you, Lord." And while you're at it, say it as often as you can any other time of the day or night.

Prayer, Love, and Feelings

At home I have a huge bowl that holds a half-gallon of ice cream and says on the side, "I love ice cream." And I use it . . . to the full.

One evening, while I was eating my beloved frozen dairy dessert from my favorite bowl, Patty asked me, "What's the difference? You love ice cream. How is it different when you tell me you love *me*?"

My spoon stopped halfway to my mouth. I pondered for a minute, then answered, "Can I get back to you on that?"

I proceeded to study every Scripture passage focusing on love, and I learned that I "loved" ice cream because it brought me pleasure. It made me feel good. And that's the way the world uses the word *love*: "I'll love you as long as you make me feel good." But biblical love is a commitment that is not dependent on emotional feeling.

Let's take this one step further, into the realm of prayer. Since prayer is an expression of love toward God and people, *our love is expressed most biblically when we pray in spite of how we feel.*

Don't wait until you feel like praying. Commit to love God and people by praying under all circumstances.

Afterward, don't determine the effectiveness of your prayers by your feelings. Good feelings will often follow when we express unconditional love through prayer, but that's not guaranteed. When you have prayed, you have told God, "I'm committed to You; I love You," no matter what emotions follow. And you can also know with confidence that you have impacted the lives of people for whom you have prayed, even if you don't feel "loving."

9. Read 1 Corinthians 13:4-8, the heart of the famous "love chapter." According to Paul's teaching here, describe the role, if any, that emotions play in the various expressions of love he lists.

10. How does the unconditional nature of loving prayer explain Paul's exhortation in Ephesians 6:18? (Note his repeated use of the words "all" and "always.")

The Next Step

The Father who loves you awaits your company. Turn to "Twenty Steps to Daily Prayer" (page 147). Try to keep the idea of your intimate companionship with God in mind as you take the next step.

Memory Passage

"Dear Friends, let us love one another, for love comes from God. Everyone who loves has been born of God and knows God."

—1 John 4:7

Going Further and Deeper

I mentioned earlier that telling God "I love you" is the most important way of coming to greater comprehension of His love for us. Let me explain another important step. This also has to do with being honest with God and expressing your inner heart to Him.

The second step to knowing the awesome love God has for you is to confess your sins.

I became a Christian at age thirteen. At that point I appropriated the sacrificial death of Jesus, and God forgave all my sins—past, present, and future (Hebrews 10:10-18; Ephesians 1:7-8; Psalm 103:12).

Why, then, should a Christian continue to confess his or her sins? It's because there are two facets to your relationship with God. *Positionally,* you are secure, safe from condemnation (Romans 8:1). But in the ongoing *personal* aspect of your relationship with God, sin hinders and damages your intimacy, and it can only be removed by confession.

For about three decades I've been married to my wife. Not for a single second of that time has our marriage relationship ceased to exist. However, there have been many occasions when I've caused offenses that have curtailed the openness and intimacy in our relationship. Each time, I have approached Patty, confessed my wrong doing, and asked her forgiveness. This is the only process by which the damage can be repaired and we can return to full enjoyment of each other.

In my relationship with God, if there's distance due to sin, I won't sense His love for me. It's only when I stop and agree with Him about my sin that I once again experience the flow of His love to me, and through me to others.

11. Study some or all of the following Scripture passages in order to understand more fully the relationship between confession of sin and our experience of God's love: Luke 7:36-47; 1 John 1:8-10, (keep in mind that this is written to Christians); Psalms 32:1-5, 66:18; Proverbs 28:13; Isaiah 1:15, 59:1-2, 64:7; Micah 3:4.

BARRIERS
TO PRAYER

～◎～

"Beware in your prayer, above everything, of limiting God, not only by unbelief, but by fancying that you know what He can do."

—Andrew Murray, pastor and author

"Fear knocked at the door. Faith answered. No one was there."

—Inscription over the mantel of Hinds' Head Hotel, England

The Danger of a Warning Unheeded

December 25, 1776, marks a day of famed courage and infamous foolishness. Throughout that night and the following morning, General George Washington rallied his depressed, underdressed troops secretly to cross the Delaware River and march upon Trenton, New Jersey, through a bone-chilling sleet storm. Trenton served as the garrison for the Hessian mercenaries under Colonel Johann Rall.

Washington's move was one of desperation and should have failed at several points. But the Americans' redemption is credited to Colonel Rall's arrogance. Rall spurned his own aides' advice to post sentries Christmas night. When a loyalist spy tried to warn Rall, the Colonel refused to see him and stuffed the man's unread note into a pocket, so as not to interrupt a poker game.

Washington attacked after daybreak on December 26. Rall was sleeping, and his three unprepared regiments panicked. Within ninety minutes, Washington won the war's first major battle with no recorded American deaths, boosting the American soldiers' morale days before thousands planned to end their enlistments and slink home in disillusionment.

Rall died the next day of wounds from the battle. While receiving medical attention, the spy's note was discovered. One of Rall's last recorded statements was, "If I had read this . . . I would not be here." (Summarized from A. J. Langguth, *Patriots*, pp. 399-419.)

On the path to disciplined prayer, we will encounter opposition that will work to defeat us. Without a healthy awareness of the obstacles, we are likely to be ambushed, taken unaware by them. In order to prevent this danger, Scripture advises us repeatedly to *stay awake*, because our opponents never rest in their efforts to thwart God's will for our lives (see "Going Further and Deeper" at the end of this lesson for further study of Scripture's warnings to stay alert).

As you study through the Scriptures and principles in this lesson, keep asking God to help you grow in alertness to the barriers to prayer in your life. In fact, why not start now? Take a moment and talk to Him.

A Hard Road to Great Reward

Before we study some common barriers to prayer, let's build the context of truths that will help us see more clearly the significance of the barriers. The first truth summarizes the main message of Lesson 1, "The Blessings of Prayer."

Truth #1:
God will bless us in proportion to our faithfulness in prayer.
The more we pray—expressing love and trust—the more He blesses.

Read Jesus' teaching in Luke 11:5-10. The original words for "ask," "seek" and "knock" in verses 9 and 10 are in a Greek tense that implies repeated, habitual, ongoing action. The same is true for "receives" and "seeks" in verse 10. In other words, Luke is recording Jesus as saying, "The one who keeps on asking will keep on receiving," and so on.

1. Describe the kind of response you hope to receive from your asking, seeking, and knocking.

2. Now describe the type of prayer habit you would expect to develop in order to receive this response.

Truth #2
There are many good things God won't do if we don't pray.

In the absence of prayer, don't expect God's blessing on your life, family, ministry, or church. In fact, you may encounter His chastisement. God greatly prefers to encourage us by promise of blessing, but, where necessary, He also warns us of His anger.

3. Read Ezekiel 22:30-31, Isaiah 59:16, and Psalm 106:23. What is one possible consequence of prayerlessness you wish to avoid?

Truth #3
Faithful, sacrificial prayer is hard to accomplish.

I once helped a friend conduct a survey in a large city, in which we polled people about spiritual matters. We found that 96 percent said they believed in God, and 98 percent in prayer. But, based on what I know of most people's prayer lives, I find it hard to believe those 98 percent had in mind the kind of persistent, sacrificial prayer Scripture describes. Such prayer is uncommon because, frankly, it's hard work. Let's examine several of the reasons that prayer is a difficult task, even though it is well worth the effort and discipline required to do it right.

Five Reasons People Don't Pray

A. Satan hates prayer and desperately tempts us with the lie that token prayer is enough. I believe prayer is the ultimate weapon against the kingdom of darkness. Second Corinthians 10:3-4 tells us that "we do not wage war as the world does. The weapons we fight with are not the weapons of the world. On the contrary, they have divine power to demolish strongholds." As I pray for individuals, one request I always include is, "Deliver them from the evil one." Prayer pushes back the kingdom of darkness, protects the people we pray for, limits Satan's work. The enemy knows that and frantically tries to convince us that prayer doesn't work, harassing and haranguing in hopes that we will wear down and give up.

I don't believe Satan is able to take control of God's people, but, as he tempted Jesus (Matthew 4:1-11), he also tempts us by lying to us in our thoughts. He schedules his attacks when we're most susceptible, and some of his lies are creative. "You're too tired," he says. "Just go to bed. You can pray tomorrow." Or, "You don't have the gift of prayer." We can be easily convinced and rationalize away our prayer life. But we need to stay alert and ask, "Where did that thought come from?" Remember, we are not struggling against flesh and blood (Ephesians 6:10-12). The kingdom of darkness is our enemy, and we need to focus our prayers against it, rather than justify casual prayer.

4. Read in Matthew 4:1-3 about the way Satan spoke to Jesus. What is one stray thought that you encounter frequently, at times when you are susceptible, which might be from the enemy? "if"

5. Read Mark 9:25-29 and Romans 16:20. Why is prayer a necessary tool in our battle against the enemy?

B. Our flesh—our sinful nature—resists every attempt our heart makes at praying. I've chosen, at the beginning of each year, to set for myself as many goals as the number of years I've lived. This year I'm fifty-four, so I've set fifty-four goals. Can you guess which one will be the most difficult? It's my goal to reduce my weight to 185 pounds. I've set that same goal each year for twenty years, and I have yet to reach it. My flesh hates to diet—it's more fun to eat. The flesh hates discipline in general, especially the regimen required for an effective prayer life.

6. According to Romans 7:15-21, what makes the difference between what I wish to do and what I actually do?

Optional: Read more of Romans 7 about this struggle, especially the hope in verses 24-25, leading to the triumph of Romans 8.

C. Sin or lukewarmness deadens the heart's appetite for prayer. Unresolved sin issues or a complacent attitude makes prayer difficult or impossible, and will eventually defeat me. When I sense the effectiveness of my prayers decreasing, I may despair and think, *What good is this? Why pray at all?* But rather than surrendering to that thought, I must deal head on with the root problem. As I confess and resolve sin, forgiveness is always immediately available. Then I can find strength to win.

7. Allow Isaiah 59:1-2 to guide you through a brief examination of your life. If there is any habitual sin or an attitude of apathy that is reducing your appetite for prayer, what is your first step toward dealing with it? (Keep in mind that it is God's grace and forgiveness that gives us the power to live a godly life—Titus 2:11-12.)

Optional: Throughout Scripture we find mentions of specific sins that hinder prayer (for example, 1 Peter 3:7; Psalm 66:18; Proverbs 28:9; Zechariah 7:12-13; Proverbs 21:13; Isaiah 59:2; Ezekiel 14:3). While you meditate on these pertinent passages, be even more alert to barriers to avoid or overcome.

D. Prayer triggers feelings of vulnerability. Prayer is, at its root, an expression of our weakness. It is, by definition, a humbling act. It's also an intimate act, opening the depths of our hearts to God, and possibly also to other people. Many people fear intimacy, even with God. This vulnerability can cause a kind of anxiety. If this happens to you, you're not alone. To better understand these emotional dynamics, and to learn practical ideas for dealing with them, see Appendix C: "Help! I'm Stuck!" (page 159).

8. How does Paul's experience in 2 Corinthians 12:7-10 help you understand how to deal with fear of vulnerability in prayer?

E. Our world system has trapped us into a frenzied lifestyle that leaves very little time for prayer. I once heard a seminar speaker claim that, in India, new believers often begin praying three hours per day. I couldn't believe it. In all my years of life and ministry, I'd never seen any new believer start out this way. During a break I challenged him on it. "It's easy to understand," he explained. "Believers in India don't own a car, a house, a dog, a lawn, a mower . . . and most don't have jobs. They have nothing else to do." It suddenly struck me that we have too much stuff, and we've been fooled into believing possessions are the ultimate good in life.

Is it wrong to own possessions? No. Is it wrong to put time into caring for our possessions? No. Is it wrong that the average believer thinks he or she is helpless to find an hour for prayer? YES! We must take a hard look at our possessions and our priorities, and ask, "What must go?" To free up some of our precious hours for prayer, we may need to sacrifice certain time-consuming activities as a love offering to God.

My creed leads me to think that prayer is efficacious, and surely days asking God to overrule all events for good is not lost. Still, there is a great feeling that when a man is praying, he is doing nothing, and this feeling makes us give undue importance to work, sometimes even to the hurrying over or even to the neglect of prayer. Do not we rest in our day too much in the arm of the flesh? Cannot the same wonders be done now as of old? Do not the eyes of the Lord run to and fro throughout the whole earth still to show Himself strong on behalf of those who put their trust in Him? Oh that God would give me more practical faith in Him! Where is now the Lord God of Elijah? He is waiting for Elijah to call on Him.

—James Gilmore of Mongolia

9. With which of the sisters in Luke 10:41-42 do you most closely identify? In your struggle over priorities, what is it that competes most strongly with prayer?

Bursting the Barriers

We've looked at both sides of the battle over our prayer lives. On one side, God promises rich blessings for faithful prayer. On the other side, the world system, the forces of darkness and our own flesh put up barriers to keep us from praying faithfully.

10. In the following diagram . . .

a. In the circle labeled "Blessings," write two or three of the blessings from Lesson 2 that you would most enjoy receiving.

b. In the rectangle labeled "Barriers," write the one or two barriers most likely to hinder you from praying faithfully (see "Going Further and Deeper" at the end of this lesson for more ideas).

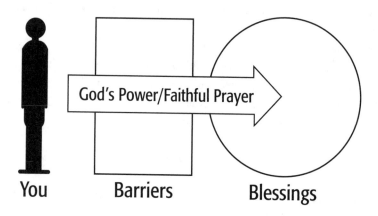

You   Barriers   Blessings

11. Now take time to talk to your Father about ways that He and you can work together to overcome the barriers between you and the blessings of prayer. Write in the space below any helpful or encouraging thoughts.

12. What will be your first step toward preventing or overcoming a barrier to prayer?

The Next Step

It's time to take your growing prayer habit to the next level. Turn to "Twenty Steps to Daily Prayer" (page 147) and launch into the next step.

Memory Passage

"His divine power has given us everything we need for life and godliness through our knowledge of him who called us by his own glory and goodness."

—2 Peter 1:3

Going Further and Deeper

13. Stay Alert!—Additional Study. *The following passages are a few of many challenging us to remain on the alert: Matthew 26:41; Acts 20:29-31; 1 Corinthians 16:13; Ephesians 6:18; Colossians 4:2; 1 Thessalonians 5:6; 1 Peter 5:8.*

Take a look at three other significant barriers to prayer:

F. Our culture has brainwashed us from birth to believe the secular, humanistic way of thinking. If people really believed in God's unconditional love and awesome power, they would pray. It's a question of values. Our culture values quick results from self-effort. But prayer is like planting corn. When I put a corn seed in the ground, I don't find a fully developed plant the next day. I need to nurture it persistently over time. Then, if I don't give up, I will see rich results. If I give up too early, I won't see any results, and the lack of fruit will mistakenly confirm the humanistic conclusion that prayer doesn't work.

14. In what ways are you tempted to tell God, "I'll believe it when I see it," as Thomas did in John 20:25?

15. What attitudes are needed in order to resist our cultural conditioning?

G. Our strong desire for comfort deceives us into accepting an easy substitute for committed, fervent, sacrificial prayer. Often, at my prayer seminars, someone will say to me, "I'm just not a Type A person. I'm not cut out for this kind of discipline." I'm frustrated by this kind of thinking. Our aversion to discipline is not a matter of temperament, but of sin nature (see Barrier B on page 53). Any effective prayer is sacrificial, and sacrifice is difficult for everyone, including me. But prayer is a critical part of every believer's life, and the Almighty has promised each of us everything we need for life and godliness (2 Peter 1:2-3).

It is true that different people are designed by God with different strengths and weaknesses. But these differing strengths don't determine whether we pray; rather, they determine how we go about praying (see Lesson 5, "Gifting and Approaches to Prayer").

16. Read Matthew 7:13-14. Honestly evaluate which aspects of your life are characterized by which path (you might live partly on each).

17. How does the assurance of 2 Peter 1:2-3 affect your response to Jesus' challenge?

H. Our pride and independence resist any appearance of weakness or begging. Again, this is a struggle with our own flesh. We'd rather *do* something and *accomplish* our way to a sense of worth. Prayer is humbling. It says, "God, I can't do anything without you," and it helps us find our sense of worth in our relationship with Him.

18. Why is it natural that Satan, described in Isaiah 14:12-14, likes it when our prideful independence flourishes?

19. How does each of the following passages help you to value and desire the humbling act of prayer? 1 Corinthians 4:7; 2 Corinthians 12:9-10; James 4:2-3,6,10.

GIFTING AND APPROACHES TO PRAYER

∽◎∾

"Always recognize that human individuals are ends,
and do not use them as means to your end."

—Immanuel Kant, German philosopher (1724-1804)

"Although the Boston Celtics have won 16 championships, they have never had
the league's leading scorer and never paid a player based on his individual
statistics. The Celtics understand that virtually every aspect of
basketball requires close collaboration."

—Robert W. Keidel, management consultant

The Kaleidoscope of Prayer

Once there was a young painter whose favorite color was green. "After all," he reasoned, "green must also be God's favorite color, since He created so much of His world in that hue." Because of his partiality, he didn't even bother purchasing any other color of paint. He began creating beautiful landscapes with forests and meadows. Then he expanded into green portraits and green abstract images, green still lifes and green sunsets. He was fully satisfied . . . until he met the artist who loved blue ("clearly God's favorite color—witness His vast canvas in the sky").

At first the green artist suspected anything to do with his new acquaintance. With time, he began to realize that blue oceans and skies looked better than those he had painted green. Amazingly, quite a number of other objects in the visual world took on new beauty when painted blue. As he broadened out into a two-color world, he thought he had achieved the ultimate in artistry . . . when Mr. and Mrs. Red moved into the neighborhood.

This story is silly, isn't it? Well, so is the way we often think of others whom God has intentionally created differently from ourselves. When it comes to prayer, many of us assume that our way is the best way, and we can be threatened by those who do it differently. Or, at least as commonly, we think in just the opposite way: *Others are spiritual giants; I could never learn to pray as they do.*

God has wisely and purposefully built a beautiful diversity into the unity of His people, and your unique gifting and personality can impact how you pray. Prayer is basically a communication vehicle we use to develop our relationship with God. The way any individual relates best to God through prayer will bear similarities to the way he or she most naturally relates to friends and family.

For example, a person who tends to be spontaneous in relationships with people is more likely to send up frequent, unplanned "arrow" prayers, as well as urgent pleas for God to fix things quickly. On the other hand, a person who is more contemplative in human relationships will most likely pray more methodically and thoughtfully.

Reality #1: *All of us find ourselves in a variety of prayer modes at various times; but each of us tends toward one set of characteristics most often.*

Reality #2: *God treasures every genuine expression of our hearts toward Him, no matter what our personality or our gifting. In fact, God continually receives a kaleidoscope of prayer, and He enjoys it as a glorious display of His own artistry.*

Celebrating Our Differences

1. Each of the following passages tells something about God's plan for diversity within the church. What implications might each passage have regarding the ways different people pray best?

1 Corinthians 12:4-7

1 Corinthians 12:8-11

1 Corinthians 12:15-26

Acknowledging each person's unique, God-given set of *personality traits* and *talent traits*, we gain fresh perspective on the reasons we pray as we do and why some methods of praying, which work for others, don't work for us. I'm convinced that God has a blueprint for each of us—for every project, job, church, city, nation—even for the future of mankind. Allow this lesson to lift you up to God's chart room, where you can see how your life fits into His larger kingdom plan. Understanding your uniqueness frees you from expecting God to follow your game plan, that you may joyfully join in with His.

Take a moment to thank your Father for His unique design in you and in others. Invite Him to show you more clearly how He has made you, and how you can best relate to Him in prayer.

Personality Traits and Prayer

Temperament or personality traits reflect a combination of God's original design for you and influences from your life experience. Let's say God designed you with a proclivity toward meeting others' needs; life experience may condition you either to be indecisive, passive, and wishy-washy, or to proactively shepherd others. The indwelling of the Holy Spirit and the healing power of the Word of God, along with the spiritual disciplines, are other influences, guiding your growth closer to God's ideal design for you in Christ. Your conscious awareness of your own personality traits will help you cooperate with God's plan to bear the fruit of maturity (Galatians 5:22-23; 1 Timothy 3:1-7).

So, let's take a look at some personality traits.

2. The pairs of listed Scripture passages illustrate each pair of contrasting traits. How does each passage demonstrate the value of each personality trait in one's relationship with God?

A. Optimistic vs. Solemn. *An optimistic person may fill his prayers with praise and gratitude, while missing out on intercession for those who are depressed or discouraged. A more solemn personality is likely to enjoy authentic expression of difficult emotions before God, but needs also to learn to climb to the heights of joy.*

1 Chronicles 29:16

Ezra 9:6

B. Assertive vs. Submissive. *The assertive pray-er is always ready to step out with decisive action, but can run ahead of God. The submissive pray-er seeks God's will carefully and obediently, but must also learn when to be assertive and proactive.*

1 Kings 18:36-38

Matthew 26:39

C. Subjective vs. Objective. *All of us are thinking and feeling beings created in the image of a thinking and feeling God. Feeling-oriented (subjective) people tend to emphasize the importance of emotion and faith-conviction in their relationship with God. These people need to consider objective facts while praying over important decisions. Fact-oriented (objective) people tend to appeal to the intellectual aspect of their relationship with God. These believers need also to give credence to the influence of the heart's emotions.*

Psalm 139:19-22

Psalm 139:23-24

D. Expressive vs. Reserved. *An expressive person's prayer allows the genuine contents of his heart to flow out to God. Prayer in groups often includes personal needs and aspirations. The prayer of the more inhibited person will likely highlight respect and reverence, tending to withhold personal disclosure.*

2 Samuel 6:14-15

Mark 12:42-44

E. Spontaneous vs. Persevering. *A persevering pray-er may find self-discipline and strength for the long haul easier to come by. But he or she sometimes fails to recognize the need for immediate, urgent action. The spontaneous pray-er may be more likely to take a risky step of obedience and faith, tending toward immediate action and intensity. But the possible danger here is lack of follow-through, especially when encountering roadblocks or God's silence.*

Matthew 14:30

Judges 6:36-40

3. Which of your personality traits do you see coming into play in your prayer life?

4. Explain how your unique personality is an asset in your relationship with God.

5. Describe one way you know you need to bring balance to your prayer life, given your natural tendencies.

Talent Traits and Prayer

Now, let's look briefly at the concept of *innate talent traits*. You may wish to use the "Going Further and Deeper" section at the end of this lesson to explore several particular talents and how they can impact one's approach to prayer. It is important to remember that talents, by definition, are given by God in whole. That means that each of us is innately gifted with aptitudes for particular skills, and it is important to discover, develop, and hone those skills with experience.

6. Read Exodus 31:1-6. What does this passage reveal about the way God distributes talents to individuals?

Throughout this study guide, I offer many specific "how-to" ideas for prayer and related disciplines. I have attempted to provide a variety of ideas for people with various personality and talent traits, but the methods I teach are naturally weighted toward the methods that work for me. In most cases, I don't apologize for this, because there are certain techniques that will benefit everyone. Please experiment and find out what works best for you. The most important thing is that you *pray* and that you pray *much.*

May God bless you as you explore prayer as an expression of your unique design. God has made you and has numbered all of your hairs (Matthew 10:30; Psalm 139). He accepts your prayers as a sweet testimony to His creative genius. You can afford to be genuine with Him in a way you may not feel you can be with anyone else.

The Next Step

Now move on to the next step in "Twenty Steps to Daily Prayer" (page 147). As you grow in prayer, focus on enjoying it according to your unique design.

Memory Passage

"There are different kinds of gifts, but the same Spirit. There are different kinds of service, but the same Lord. There are different kinds of working, but the same God works all of them in all men."

—1 Corinthians 12:4-6

Going Further and Deeper

Here are several talent traits and the ways they relate to your prayer life.

Word usage and communication talents. Some people are especially gifted with words, written or spoken. When these people pray out loud, their prayers sound effortlessly eloquent. Depending partly on the attitude of the person praying, these words may inspire or intimidate. A person with these talents must yield them to God for His constructive use.

By the way, for those who do not possess these talents, the more time you spend reading Scripture, particularly the Psalms and the prophets, the more you will learn to pray with verbal power. There is power in praying God's words back to Him, so don't be embarrassed about using Scripture as a script. Also there are several published resources that provide suggested prayers to use as a starting point.

Music. Singing or instrumental music adds a wonderful dimension to prayer—private or corporate. What are most worship songs but prayers put to music? Purely instrumental music can be an expression of praise to God, both for the performing artist and for listeners.

Art. Dare I repeat the adage, "A picture is worth a thousand words"? Yes, art is a form of communication, and since God gave that gift to some of us, we can use it to communicate our hearts to Him and to lead others toward God. Look around and see how God has expressed Himself to us through His artistic creativity. Any artistic form can be an avenue for praise, an expression of joy to God. Consider, as a devotional exercise, creating some work of art with God in mind.

Timeliness and orderliness. Some of us naturally use time efficiently and keep things in their place. Such a person prefers an established format or structure for prayer, such as liturgy. Also, time efficiency can help us make time for God in the midst of a busy week. Some of us are not gifted in this area, but all of us must learn to create enough order to keep God's priorities—Himself especially—at the top of the list.

Creativity and imagination. A person with these talents may enjoy a free flowing prayer format, with no particular direction or order. His mind may "ping pong" from thought to unrelated thought. Keeping a prayer journal may help him find connections within the flood of thoughts, and can also free him from fear of losing one thought as he moves on to another. Creative people like to experiment and innovate rather than follow standardized or "routine" patterns, such as liturgical prayer.

Entrepreneurism. Most entrepreneurs are individuals who take action; they see an opportunity and move on it. Such people easily become frustrated with share-and-wait prayer. But even these movers and shakers can find fresh value in prayer by keeping a prayer journal and letting their prayer times flow out into a list of goals. As you regularly submit your heart to God, you will find yourself thinking more like He does. You will begin to understand more clearly His wisdom and vision for the goals He sets before you, both in the small, daily matters, and in large, life-long pursuits. Resist the temptation to expect God to catch up with you. Instead, humbly recognize He is the one in the lead, showing the way.

Managing and planning. These two distinct traits reflect a heart of stable leadership. These people require predictable circumstances and are not attracted to spontaneous or new start-up activities. A planner seeks to look way into the future and may enjoy rich results from praying in that direction. A person gifted at managing is concerned with the cooperation of all concerned in the pursuit of a goal and therefore will be supportive of interpersonal cooperation. This person may have a prayer burden for relational unity and harmony among believers.

Helping and nurturing. What a gift God has provided in those special saints who bring soothing oil to our hurts! Their prayers of compassion and mercy can cause supernatural healing and restoration, both emotional and physical. Their greatest fulfillment is in finding and helping those who are hurting and who need encouragement. We are all instructed to pray for each other, but these people are especially gifted at intercession.

Promoting and motivating. Some people are bursting to tell anyone about their latest project, "deal," book or restaurant. They champion any worthy cause and eagerly update others with the latest news. These people's prayers, particularly their audible prayers with others, can become a platform for persuasion. This can be annoying if it merely seems pushy. But a persuasive person with a genuine passion for God can bring a sense of urgency and strength to a dull prayer meeting.

Problem solving and analyzing. Some of us are deep thinkers. We like to look underneath and identify causes or root issues. Consequently, a time of prayer will be most meaningful when there is that corresponding depth of reflection and conversation with God about the "whys" of His dealings and our experience. We must stop short of arrogant demands to know, but sometimes God provides insight, both for the thoughtful pray-er and for others, with whom the pray-er can share his insights.

Character intuition. Some people are extremely intuitive and can "read" people quickly. Those with this talent may be bothered when praying with others in whom they perceive insincere motives. But they can also turn their talent to constructive ends, praying for God's working in people's hearts, where perhaps no one else knows there is a need.

7. In each of the following examples of prayer, which talent traits do you see at work? (Genesis 18:23-32; Daniel 6:10; Psalm 32:1-7; Acts 1:23-26; Ephesians 1:15-19)

8. Where did you see yourself as you read through the preceding talent descriptions? What valuable contributions might your talents bring to your prayer life?

9. Think about others who have talents that are different from yours—talents, perhaps, that you haven't understood or appreciated. How might they uniquely contribute to your life or to others' lives through prayer?

Lesson 6

WHAT TO PRAY FOR PEOPLE

∽ලෙ

"Those who always pray are necessary to those who never pray."

—Victor Hugo, French author (1802-1885)

"If you are planning for one year, grow rice. If you are planning for 20 years, grow trees. If you are planning for centuries, grow men."

—Chinese proverb

We Need Each Other!

My job for many years involved working with dynamite and heavy road construction equipment. This was dangerous work, and we lived by one hard and fast rule—never work alone. Two people together were more likely to spot deadly mistakes that a lone worker might overlook.

God has set up a similar rule in the body of Christ. His design is that we become interdependent, in order to support and encourage each other, to exercise our strengths where others are weak, to spot dangers a brother or sister might not see.

The loving commitment of prayer is key to this dynamic. I believe that prayers for others carry more power than prayers for ourselves, that we need each others' prayer more than we need to be praying for our own needs. Prayer is not an inconsequential activity; God actually changes lives because we pray. In fact, you can have greater impact in another person's life by praying for him than through anything else you might do for him.

So, let's say you're convinced that praying for others is important. Your next question might be, "What do I pray?" In this lesson we'll look at a few specifics Scripture provides, that indicate we should all regularly pray for each other.

But before we do, an important side note: As we saw in Lesson 5, no two of us are exactly the same. In my own practice, I'm able to pray the same requests repeatedly for many people without the process becoming boring or the repeated requests becoming meaningless. When I am aware of other specific needs, I will add requests that are unique to each person. Your prayer pattern may very well differ from mine. The requests we will study in this lesson serve as the foundation of your prayer ministry for people. I encourage you to build on this foundation in whatever way is best suited and most meaningful to you.

Praying for Fellow Believers

A. Pray for spiritual growth and mature, Christlike character. I've become so convinced of my prayers' impact on people's hearts that I sometimes physically ache with anticipation for what God will do. You can cultivate this same passion and confidence, especially as you see God bearing fruit in people's lives, in response to your prayers.

1. Give one or two specific examples of the kind of change you would see in the lives of the people you care about as you pray each of the following prayers for them.

Colossians 4:12

2 Corinthians 13:9

1 Thessalonians 5:23

In these Scripture passages, "mature and fully assured" or similar wording actually comes from different Greek words in each passage. In Colossians 4:12, Paul uses the adjective *teleios,* which literally means "taken all the way to its end," and refers not to literal perfection, but rather to maturity or completeness. In 2 Corinthians 13:9, he uses the noun *katartisis,* referring to complete qualification or matured ability due to training. And in 1 Thessalonians 5:23, behind the phrase "sanctify you through and through," we find *holoteleis,* a merging of the word *holos,* "whole, entire," and *teleios* (described above), together meaning "through and through, altogether;" and in the phrase "be kept blameless," we find *holokleros,* "whole, intact, in all aspects."

B. Pray that they would overcome sin. Our greatest weapon in the battle for souls is prayer. God's power in response to our prayers will always overwhelm sin's power.

2. Why is the prayer of 2 Corinthians 13:7 one you believe God can and will answer?

that you will do no evil —
— that you would do what is honorable

3. What additional confidence does 1 Corinthians 10:13 add to your prayers for yourself and others?

make a way of escape

C. Pray that they would know the will of God for their lives. Many believers do not even understand the will of God clearly pointed out in Scripture. As a starting point, pray that their lives would begin to reflect what God says in His Word. Next, when you know people who are wrestling with important decisions, pray that God's will would become clear to them.

4. According to Joshua 1:8, what is God's definition of success?

observe to do all that is written in it

5. *Summarize in your own words the request Paul makes and the results from God's response in Colossians 1:9-10.*

filled with the knowledge of His will — — wisdom and spiritual understanding

D. Pray for protection from the devil. This is especially appropriate for leaders, including parents. While there are certainly many ways we may protect people, prayer calls upon the power and love of God—the strongest shield anyone could ask for.

6. *How is the attitude of 1 Peter 5:8 an attitude of power and confidence, rather than one of paranoia? (See also the verses just before and after.)*

humbly under the hand of God all cares cast on Him, sober and vigilant resisting, steadfast in the faith

7. *How can you regularly incorporate Jesus' prayer of John 17:15 into your prayer routine?*

Keep them from the evil one

E. Pray for deliverance from the world's temptations, that they might not fall away from God. Many believers are derailed spiritually because they fall into temptation. We are even instructed by Jesus, in the Lord's Prayer, to pray against temptation. And remember what Jesus said to Peter: "Satan has asked to sift you as wheat. But I have prayed for you, Simon, that your faith may not fail" (Luke 22:31).

8. *What does 1 John 2:15 mean by "love" for the world and its things?*

firm attachment and attraction

9. *How can you become actively involved in the continuation of Jesus' protective ministry toward those in your life (John 17:11-12)?*

pray - keep through Your name

F. Pray that they would be bold, effective witnesses for Jesus. It's tough to be bold in our witness of the gospel. Even the apostle Paul struggled in this area. He asked the Ephesian believers to "pray also for me, that whenever I open my mouth, words may be given me so that I will fearlessly make known the mystery of the gospel" (Ephesians 6:19).

believe it

10. How can your prayer ministry change people's attitudes toward their entire purpose for earthly existence (John 17:18)?

11. In John 17:20, Jesus acknowledged that your salvation is a direct result of His prayer for His men's witnessing power (also 17:6-19)! What fruit might be borne for centuries to come if you pray for fellow believers (and yourself) to witness boldly for Christ?

Take a few minutes and offer several of these requests to God on behalf of at least one or two believing friends or family members. Put these requests into your own words, and thank God now for His answers.

Praying for Unbelievers

The apostle Paul veritably burned with desire to see people brought into God's kingdom, setting his life on the line for them time after time. But Paul could have sacrificed his life a thousand times over, and it would never have done as much for the lost as when he called on the power of Almighty God. This is why he wrote, in Romans 10:1: "My heart's desire and prayer to God for the Israelites is that they may be saved."

We pray to the same God Paul did, and when we pray, God literally changes the world. Not only can our prayers impact the lives of unbelievers, but the practice of disciplined prayer will impact our own hearts as well. As we invest time praying for the lost, we will begin to see them with the eyes of God, and our passion will grow.

A. Pray that the Holy Spirit will convict your friends of sin. Before anyone can appreciate the cure, he must respect the disease. Acceptance of the bad news leads to gratitude for the good news.

12. Read at least two of these passages: John 16:7-8; Acts 2:37; Jude 14-15; Luke 18:10-14. How can God positively use conviction of sin?

B. Pray that God will produce in your friends a growing fear of death, fear of God, fear of judgment, and a realization that life is short. This may *bring this to the LORD*

seem cruel, but the enemy loves to keep his victims complacent regarding these life-and-death matters. Only God's grace will wake people up to the danger they truly face.

13. *Why is it healthy to understand our own limitations (Hebrews 9:27; Psalms 90:10-12, 39:4)?*

14. *How is it possible to fear God and love Him at the same time (Proverbs 1:7; Luke 12:5)?*

an awesome reverence includes fear

C. Pray for a growing hunger for joy and a realization that heaven is real. This request and the next one reflect the positive side of all that God offers through salvation. People are naturally hungry to have these needs met, because God has designed each of us with these needs.

15. *Read John's description of heaven in Revelation 21:1-7 and 22:1-5 (optional: Isaiah 35:10; 1 Corinthians 2:9; Psalm 27:4). How does this picture change your perception of the world around you?* *add vs 5 NLT*

D. Pray that God will deepen their desire for a close personal relationship with Himself. At the heart of salvation and heaven is the Person of God Himself. Every heart's deepest longing is for right relationship with our Creator, who made us in His image.

16. *Why is prayer critical in order for people to want what they so desperately need (Jeremiah 29:13; Romans 3:11; John 6:44)?*

E. Pray that God will open the eyes of their hearts to understand the truth of the gospel. Satan wants to keep people blinded to the truth. Pray that God's light would shine in the hearts of those for whom you are praying.

17. Why must God intervene in order for people to clearly see the truth (2 Corinthians 4:4; Acts 16:14; Luke 24:45; Ephesians 1:18)?

*urgent prayer: pray that they will have a confident hope.
only hope prevents dispair and suicide*

F. Pray for an opportunity to serve your friends and to genuinely love them by meeting needs. Then keep your eyes and mind open to see ways to show love. This is love through action.

18. Paul loved people through action (1 Corinthians 9:19-22, 10:24,33). What actions might speak love to your unbelieving friends?

G. Pray for the opportunity to share what Jesus means to you. This is love through truthful words.

19. How will praying help prepare you for the opportunities God will provide (Colossians 4:2-3)?

H. Pray that your friends would say "yes" when you invite them to church or other opportunities to learn of Jesus. Remember, it is never your job to create a response or a commitment in someone else. That is God's job. Yours is to share the truth and to cultivate a loving, safe environment.

20. How does God intend the behavior of believers toward each other to be an instrument for outreach purposes (John 13:35; 17:20-21)?

Special note: Be sure also to pray for yourself, for real love and desire for your friends' salvation (see Paul's and Jesus' examples in Romans 9:1-3 and Matthew 9:36-38). Pray for your own boldness to speak (Acts 4:31). Don't be afraid of mistakes. You will make them, but God will still use you and you will develop skill through the experience.

Take time now to offer a number of these requests, in your own words, on behalf of a few unbelieving friends or family members. Enjoy thinking about the prospect of God's answers.

The Next Step
As you take the next step in "Twenty Steps to Daily Prayer" (page 147) allow yourself a special emphasis on prayer for people throughout the week.

Memory Passage
"Devote yourselves to prayer, being watchful and thankful."

—Colossians 4:2

Going Further and Deeper

Does Repetition Seem Mechanical?
It's only human to find a request fading into meaninglessness as we repeat it over and over. But Scripture teaches us to pray persistently and importunately. This is the type of prayer Jesus advocated (Luke 11:5-10, 18:1-8). Is it possible to obey such instruction and, at the same time, to keep repetition from becoming meaningless drudgery?

Yes, we can learn to pray with meaningful repetition. After all, isn't a married person or a parent able to tell his spouse or child "I love you" with meaning, time after time, day after day, for years on end? Of course, for some, even this phrase can lose its meaning, but there are millions of marriages and families who are living proof that the phrase can sustain meaning through thousands of repetitions.

So, how do we keep repetitious prayers meaningful? First, commit to purposefully engage your mind and heart in your prayers every time you pray. Ask God to keep your mind from wandering and to keep your heart fervently involved in the words you speak to Him. Then even the most repeated requests can sustain their significance in your mind.

Second, watch for God's answers to your requests—especially those you repeat most often. This will help you believe more strongly in the power and willingness of God to answer your repeated requests, and so you will pray them with greater faith.

Third, work at remaining aware of spiritual realities. Remind yourself often of the true spiritual danger from the evil one and his demonic army. Meditate on the existence, power, love, and wisdom of God, who hears and answers your prayers. Never stop believing in people's potential for supernatural growth and impact in the world, as God answers your prayers for them. When we live constantly in a growing awareness of the spiritual world and the spiritual battle, all of our requests will take on new significance, and the most repeated requests will become the ones for which we feel the greatest passion.

Stop now and talk once again to your Father. Ask Him to provide you with the commitment to remain healthily persistent in prayer, growing in fervency and passion. If specific ideas are beginning to formulate in your mind about the particular daily and weekly habits of prayer you want to develop, write them down as tentative commitments.

PASSION— HUNGER FOR GOD

∼◉∽

"When thou prayest, rather let thy heart be without words

than thy words without heart."

—John Bunyan, English preacher (1628-1688)

"He prays well who is so absorbed with God that he does not know he is praying."

—Francis de Sales, Bishop of Geneva (1567-1622)

"Age quid agis, says the Latin: Do what you do. Be in earnest, and do not trifle."

—Charles Spurgeon, English preacher (1834-1892)

What Do You Feed Your Passion?

For thousands of years cultures around the world have attempted to locate the human soul within the body. The heart, liver, and brain have all been proposed as the soul's home. Some have believed the soul to be distributed evenly just under the skin. Others have concluded that the soul is not related to any physical body part.

There's another critically important component in the human being. I like to call it the "wanter." I don't know where it's located, but I know a little about the way it works. The wanter functions well and becomes incredibly strong when we feed it by desiring the right things—namely, God and His values. But the wanter weakens and loses its appetite when it is exercised toward evil desires. Even permissible desires and life necessities, such as money, food, and relationships can have a harmful effect if they become our wanter's central focus.

It is healthy to want . . . to want really bad . . . to want so much it hurts. You are most spiritually healthy when you want God so much that you are totally consumed. Getting out of bed is easy. Giving yourself away fills you with satisfaction, not self-pity. You accomplish as much life as you can in a day. And at day's end, you don't think, *Poor me,* but rather, *This is living! Bring on more . . . tomorrow!*

Another name for the wanter is "passion." Passion is critical to achieving success in life. Everyone is capable of passion, and without it, no believer can live the abundant life God promises.

How's Your Appetite?

Many believers have lost their passion to accomplish anything significant. They hide in quiet mediocrity. They fool themselves and others into believing that such "safe" living is good, using biblical terminology like "humility," "contentment," and "faithfulness," rather than more accurate terms, such as "apathy," "fear," and "disobedience." They are far from the cutting edge of usefulness in God's hand.

Most tragically, without passion prayer becomes meaningless. And, conversely, without fervent prayer, passion withers. I often beg for God to keep passion fresh in my heart. When believers lose their passion, they become walking dead (Revelation 3:1).

Why does a believer lose his or her passion, that inner fire that drives us to accomplish great things for God? That's a question I'll answer later in this lesson, under "Going Further and Deeper: Killers of Passion."

1. In your own words, what is implied as God's highest desire for every believer in Revelation 3:15-16?

2. Both Jacob (Genesis 32:24-28) and the blind men (Matthew 20:29-33) displayed strong, reckless passion. Describe one way you would benefit by following their examples.

3. In your own words, what does Psalm 37:4 tell us to do in order to have a heart that wants what God desires?

When you want a lot, you pray a lot, because wanting leads you to the feet of the One who can provide all things. The more you want, the more you work in cooperation with God to achieve those wants—both for His sake and for your own sake—because both God and man are blessed when God's will is accomplished on earth. The more you want, the more you dream, and the more goals you set. Some people will be attracted to your dreams, but be prepared for those with little spiritual appetite to think you're strange, because of your passion.

Desires that Feed Your Passion

The surgeon general seeks to educate Americans about the "food pyramid," that we might feed our bodies properly. Let's seek out what Scripture teaches about a healthy diet for our passion.

A. Desire to know and love God. This is the highest, purest and noblest longing of all, and all other godly desires spring out of it. Enjoy your present relationship with God to its fullest, but never allow yourself to plateau and stagnate. Anyone who says they've come to know God as fully as they can is deceived. With Paul, let's say, "I want to know you, Lord, and I'll give up anything in life to that end."

4. Read Philippians 3:7-8. As God increasingly takes center stage in your heart, what other objects of desire will be pushed aside?

5. How does your passion for God compare with the standard set in Psalms 42:1-2, 73:25, 143:6; Isaiah 26:9?

This is an excellent place in our study to stop and consider afresh your relationship with the God,

- who skillfully and lovingly created you.
- who provides your every need.
- who sacrificed His Son for you.
- who zealously pursues you for Himself.
- who has chosen you and adopted you as His own child.

Consider the passion He has displayed toward you, for your unbelievable good. Talk with Him about it. Then talk with Him about your passion toward Him and how strong you want it to become. Finally, meditate on the truth that this is the request He most strongly longs to grant you.

B. Desire for holiness and righteousness. We've all learned that, no matter how successfully we might attain to Christ's righteous character, we will always be approaching, never arriving. Praise God for your growth, but don't become satisfied with your progress to date. The heart of passion always wants more of God's holiness and righteousness.

6. How can you keep fostering unquenchable desire for holiness without becoming discouraged that you haven't arrived (Matthew 5:6; 1 Peter 1:14-16)?

C. Desire for wisdom. You can't become too wise. I plead for wisdom daily (2 Chronicles 1:7-12).

7. What might the pursuit of wisdom look like in your life (Proverbs 2:2-5, 3:13-18)?

8. How might your last week have been different if you believed with unshakable confidence the promise of James 1:5?

D. Desire to see people come to Jesus. Our longing for the salvation of unbelievers is _driven by God's love within us_ and should never be satisfied until there is not a single lost person (see Lesson 6, "What to Pray for People").

9. What might cause your desire for people's salvation to fall short of the passion of Paul (Romans 9:1-3, 10:1) and Jesus (Luke 13:34)?

10. What rights or comforts might you need to sacrifice in order to see people into God's eternal kingdom (1 Corinthians 9:19-27)?

E. Desire for your family, ministry, and church to be healthy, loving, and unified. Have you even scratched the surface of all you can achieve if you, together, were to avail yourselves of all the blessings God has in store for you? Always long for more . . . together!

11. Ephesians 5:25-27 serves as a model for our own attitude toward the church. How can you strengthen and pursue your desire for loving, unified relationships between believers?

F. Desire for much spiritual fruit and great accomplishments for the glory of God. Our church is fairly large. Yet I intend to draw more people to Christ and to build up more believers. I'd like to send more people onto the mission field. I strive for a higher percentage of solid families and marriages in our body. I'd like to plant another daughter church. The desire to make a greater impact for God is pure and right.

One evening recently, I was sitting exhausted at home, and a thought arose: *Duke, if you would just be content, you could slow down, stop praying so much, throttle back a little. You're fifty-four!* I entertained the idea for only a moment. Then the last dozen years' experience overwhelmed this puny temptation. The "safe" life is my worst horror. I'd rather die than give up the exciting blessings of the last decade plus. Even greater adventures await! Why stop now? I'll keep wanting more blessing, more of the kingdom, more of God's glory, until the day I die.

12. In John 15:7-8, what are the conditions ("if" statements) for asking what we wish? What does this say about our relationship with God?

13. Why does such prayer, and the fruit borne of it, bring God pleasure?

14. How might you imitate the desires of Jabez (1 Chronicles 4:10)?

The stronger the passion, the more you pray; and the more you pray, the stronger the passion. Devotion to prayer gets you in touch with God's dreams for yourself, your family, your church, your community, your world. God's desires become your desires, consuming you, as you spend time with Him in prayer.

That passion will attract people to you and to your dreams. It will inspire confidence in those under your care. Passion guides your every waking thought and deed, gives you reason to gladly make sacrifices. You adopt a new value system, a worldview that is alien to the passionless, but that is thoroughly familiar to God and those closest to Him. Trivial things stop mattering. Steps of obedience that used to "seriously inconvenience" you now become small prices to pay for God's glory. Setbacks and losses become manageable, hurdles on the road to that which consumes you.

Passion ignites this mindset and causes it to burn brighter, until you blaze for the Lord, attracting people from miles around to the spectacle. You will set fire to some of them. While Jesus spits lukewarm believers out of His mouth (Revelation 3:16), He delights in the longing heart. This is the heart God wants in all of us, and it will grow as you pray.

15. How would you describe the level of your passion? Why?

Talk with your Father about your passion. Invite His evaluation, and ask Him for insight as to what drives you and what holds you back. Thank Him for passion He has given you, and confess to Him any hindrances. Ask for more passion and for wisdom as you move on.

Finally, write here at least one specific goal that will help ignite your passion or cause it to burn more brightly. Put this goal on a card to carry with you, and read it each day for the next four weeks. Pray each day that God will help you reach that goal. Then watch what happens.

The Next Step

Turn now to "Twenty Steps to Daily Prayer" (page 147) and free yourself to dream as you take the next step.

Memory Passage

> "But whatever was to my profit I now consider loss for the sake of Christ. What is more, I consider everything a loss compared to the surpassing greatness of knowing Christ Jesus my Lord, for whose sake I have lost all things. I consider them rubbish, that I may gain Christ."
>
> —Philippians 3:7-8

Going Further and Deeper

Killers of Passion

A. Wrong desires. My dad died of cancer. There was a point, as the disease grew, when he lost his appetite for food. Mom begged him to eat, but the end was clearly near. For us spiritually, loss of appetite for the good things of God is a sign that some degree of spiritual death has set in. When we lose the desire for success, achievement, and fruit bearing, it is likely due to the inappropriate exercise of our passion toward greedy desires. Wrong desires kill good desires.

When we want the wrong things—objects our passion was not designed to desire—our passion weakens. It atrophies and shrivels, like an unused muscle. When we want nothing, we stop praying. What is there worth asking for? We become apathetically satisfied with the mere sustenance of life. This happens even when we let permissible but lesser desires become central, pushing out true godly desires.

16. Describe the dismal sequence of events leading to the loss of one's spiritual appetite (Mark 4:19; Ecclesiastes 2:10-11; Numbers 11:4-6).

B. Misplaced contentment. What I am about to say may shock you: Contentment is very bad. Never, never be content. The more you receive from God and achieve for God, the less content you ought to be.

Now let me clarify: I'm speaking about contentment with a spiritual plateau, where you stop reaching for God and all the pursuits that bring Him glory. On the other hand, it is right to be content with earthly things (finances, house, car). The world is discontent with the wrong things, with the objects that serve us only in this life. In contrast, the world is quite apathetic toward anything of eternal worth.

17. How does Paul clarify appropriate and inappropriate contentment in Philippians 4:11-12 and 1 Timothy 6:6-9?

C. Fear of failure. As our passion grows, we encounter risks. The greater the desire, the greater the pain if it isn't fulfilled. Fear of disappointment and failure tempts us to throttle back on our passion, but the wise man thwarts that temptation and begs God to fill him with passion. We are each destined for disappointment and pain, but the gains to be achieved through passion for God far outweigh the losses. In fact, even pain is a good thing, when allowed by God as part of His maturing process (James 1:2-4; 1 Peter 1:6-9). Greater passion, greater achievement, and greater blessing will result.

Fear of failure will lead to less prayer, less effort, less servanthood, fewer sacrifices . . . and less blessing. God save me from such a fate!

18. In what pursuits of your life do you identify most strongly with the fears of the unfaithful steward in Matthew 25:24-30?

D. Comparison with others. It's possible for desire for godly success to subtly transform into dissatisfaction, due to jealousy over someone else's success. The object of one's desire shifts from God's values to a worldly one-upmanship, and misplaced desire kills passion. The heart becomes apathetic, weary and dry, content with mediocrity.

19. Read 2 Corinthians 10:12. What insecurities within you might cause you to play the comparison game?

E. Mistreatment of your physical body. Our bodies and spirits are integrated and influence each other. Poor diet and lack of rest or exercise can lower our energy levels and hinder our spiritual passion. I can't become passionate without the right amount of sleep. It's simply the way we're designed. Even Jesus recognized this.

20. In what ways did Jesus acknowledge the need to care for the body in order to live with passion (Matthew 8:24, 14:13; Mark 6:31)?

Part 2

SPECIAL
TOPICS

STRATEGIES FOR PRAYING IN YOUR AREA OF INFLUENCE (FAMILY OR MINISTRY)

∼◦∼

"The best way for a child to learn to fear God is to know a real Christian. The best way for a child to learn to pray is to live with a father and mother who know a life of friendship with God, and who truly pray."

—Johann Heinrich Pestalozzi, Swiss educator (1746-1827)

prayer

"Let us diligently apply the means, never doubting that a just God, in His own good time, will give us the rightful result."

—Abraham Lincoln, 16th U.S. president, (1809-1865)

If the Price Is Right...

When I turned fifty, my doctor said, "Dee, you're going to die." "Of course, we're all going to die," I replied. "No," he said, "I mean soon. Unless you start immediately to exercise, diet, and lose a significant amount of weight, your days are numbered." He had my attention.

Recently I went to my dentist. The hygienist began to lecture about flossing, and I gave my usual excuses, until she explained the alternatives. If I wanted to keep my teeth the rest of my life, I would floss. If I wanted them all to fall out within a decade or so, I could keep on believing my excuses. She had my attention.

Each of these health care professionals did an excellent job of selling me on an idea. Part of their job was to persuade me to do what was in my own best interest, and now I regularly floss and I regularly jog.

As a spiritual leader, it's your job to sell your people on an idea, to persuade them to adopt a discipline that will only do them good. It's one thing to become an individual devoted to prayer. It's another to lead a family, ministry, or church that is given to disciplined prayer.

This lesson presents a number of strategies I've found helpful, as a husband, father, and pastor, for fostering a group commitment to prayer. You'll find more ideas than you can implement at once, so watch for the few most strategic ideas for your family or ministry. I'll point out the strategies that I think are most important to start with.

Editor's Note: For editorial purposes, the noun "leader" is used throughout this chatper. Whether or not you are a leader in your church doesn't matter. You can apply these principles in praying for any area of influence—family, work, etc.

Twelve Strategies for Leaders

A. You, the leader, need to pray a lot. Those under your care will seldom rise above your commitment level; you are their example. Howard Hendricks said, "If you want people to bleed, you have to hemorrhage." You need not be a spiritual giant; simply walk ahead of your people in humble obedience. If the leader won't make the time and sacrifices to lead, who will?

1. Read Acts 6:1-4. The Jerusalem leaders were not above waiting on tables, but they recognized the strategic nature of leaders' prayers for their people. How will your devotion to prayer enhance the other aspects of your leadership and ministry?

2. From the following passages, list the words and phrases that described Paul's prayer life as a leader: Ephesians 1:16; Romans 1:9-10a; 1 Thessalonians 3:10; 2 Timothy 1:3.

3. Whether you're a leader or not, how can your prayer model become a ministry to others (1 Peter 5:2-3; Philippians 3:17)?

B. Pray faithfully for the people under your care. This is the most important strategy in this entire lesson, because prayer is the most loving thing you can do for others. Start praying faithfully and systematically for people (keeping a list helps most people). Your prayers will impact those people's lives more greatly than anything else you do for them.

4. Some think Jethro's primary advice in Exodus 18:17-21 was that Moses delegate his work to others. But what was actually first on Moses' job description (18:19-21)? Why is this significant to you?

5. Read Colossians 1:9-11. This is a prayer God loves to answer. Choose three of Paul's phrases and describe what will happen for the people under your care as God fulfills each one. ask God to show them His will
spiritual wisdom & understanding
their lives will come to honor & please the Lord
their lives produce fruit
they will be strengthened by His power
they will have endurance and patience with joy

C. Recruit people to pray for you as leader. This is the second most important strategy. Ask a few individuals, preferably from your family or ministry, to pray for your leadership effectiveness. You'll find confidence and security in the face of an enemy who targets leaders.

> "The most underutilized source of spiritual power in our churches today is intercession for Christian leaders. I purposely did not say 'one of the most underutilized sources of power' because I do not think anything else this important is actually so neglected."
>
> —C. Peter Wagner, *Prayer Shield*

6. Read Colossians 4:2-3, Ephesians 6:18-19, and 2 Corinthians 1:11 to see how Paul recruited others to pray for him and his ministry. What do you want people to pray for you?

Here is a list of requests I ask people to pray for me:

- Preaching (or other ministry responsibilities)
- Protection from Satan
- Power to endure emotionally
- Passion for God and His values
- People skills, that I might know how to love each person
- Priorities
- Perception or wisdom, that I might know God's will

D. Make a firm commitment to a specific plan, and make yourself accountable. Most individuals or groups that fail to maintain devotion to prayer do so either for lack of a specific plan or failure to take the plan seriously. Accountability is critical; we were never designed to remain disciplined alone. Accountability requires humility, which is often misdefined as saying, "I can't do it," when it really means, "I can't do it by myself" (see Lesson 10, "Accountability that Works").

E. Pray frequently with the people under your care. This reaps many benefits. For one, when I'm praying with others, my private prayer life thrives. Also, those who pray together share a spiritual intimacy unparalleled through almost any other means. (Because of this, I prefer that non-family prayer groups be same-sex. Never be involved in an ongoing situation where you are praying with one person of the opposite sex—unless that person is your spouse, child, or sibling.)

7. How can praying with others serve as an opportunity for mutual education (Luke 11:1, 9:28)?

8. Read at least three of these passages, and list the words and phrases that describe the corporate (group) prayer life of the early church: Acts 1:14, 2:42-44, 4:24, 12:5,12, 20:36.

F. Keep prayer as a topic regularly before those in your sphere of influence. Bring up prayer in discussion, teaching, Bible study, and other communications. I like to say, "Boil water." The second you remove heat from boiling water, it stops boiling. Lovingly keep the heat on those in your care to keep them faithfully praying. Learn to be creatively repetitious.

9. What form might Paul's "urging" (1 Timothy 2:1) have taken?

10. How does Paul's advocacy of a multifaceted teaching approach (2 Timothy 4:2) apply in your situation?

G. Teach your people to become goal setters and to make and keep specific commitments. No matter how much head knowledge a person has attained, all growth takes place at the point of commitment to action or change. People tend to avoid commitments and goals, because they're disappointed with past failures. We'll look at ways to turn these failures into successes in Lesson 11.

11. Acts 3:1 tells of a specific prayer commitment that was common to all Israel and maintained by the early church. What difference might such commitments make in your situation?

H. Set regular times for your family or ministry members to pray together. Make use of already established patterns and habits. Attach prayer sessions to already planned gatherings, or replace some event with prayer. Starting with even three people is worthwhile. Take care to teach everyone corporate prayer etiquette (see Lesson 9).

I. Hang out with passionate people to keep your passion hot. It is the leader's responsibility to stay fired up for God and for prayer. You'll be inspired by some people's passion through their books or tapes. I listen to sermon tapes or books on tape while I jog.

J. Expose your people to excellent prayer resources, such as those mentioned in the preceding point. Be prepared to invest part of your budget to this end. The return is well worthwhile.

K. Regularly encourage story sharing, especially by those who have seen prayers answered, whose lives have been changed by prayer.

L. Never give up. Keep boiling the water. Motivating your people to commit and to maintain their commitment may be one of the most difficult things you'll ever do. But the end result will pay rich dividends. Don't give up, and together you will make a difference beyond all proportion to your ability. You'll see God at work.

Shortly before my dad's military retirement, we lived in Alameda, California. My dad would take us kids down to the dock to fish. One day a huge battleship was tied up to the dock, dwarfing all of us. Without warning, Dad stepped to the edge, his toes extending over the water, and he leaned out at a forty-five-degree angle in order to push with all his might against the ship. We began to think Dad should have started retirement sooner. Despite our bewildered glances and disparaging gestures, Dad kept pushing against the huge ship. For fifteen or twenty minutes he pushed, with no result. Finally, to our amazement, the ship moved! At that moment I would not have been surprised to see a big, red "S" on Dad's chest.

Sitting down with us on the dock, Dad said, "I didn't make it through much school, and I'm not sure how this works. But somehow my energy is stored in that ship, as I push. After a while there's enough energy that it moves. Now, never forget two things. First, if I had quit even two seconds too soon, it wouldn't have moved, and all I had done up to that point would have been wasted. And second, if one of you had helped me, we would have done it in half the time."

This is now my mental image for moving groups of people to pray. Keep pushing, in love. If one other person will push with you, recruit them, and both of you keep pushing. If you don't give up, you will see results. It is God's will that families and ministries be devoted to prayer, and national revival may well begin with you.

12. Jesus taught this same attitude of persistence in Luke 18:1 and following. How will you keep the water boiling in your situation?

13. Review the strategies in this lesson (see also the additional strategies under "Going Further and Deeper"), and mark with a check any you already have in place. These need continued maintenance, but you can build on them. If you check few or none, don't feel badly. You know right where to start.

14. Now circle the most important few (between two and six) that you want to focus on first. Pray as you make your decisions, taking even a day or two. Be sure to include Strategies B and C if you are not already using them.

15. Once you have made your choices, pray over the specific ways you will implement these strategies. As action steps come to mind, write them below or on separate paper. Where appropriate, include steps for presenting these strategies to your people.

The Next Step

Continue your progress to the next step in "Twenty Steps to Daily Prayer" (page 147). Your progress and growth is important in your ministry to those you love.

Memory Passage

"On him we have set our hope that he will continue to deliver us, as you help us by your prayers. Then many will give thanks on our behalf for the gracious favor granted us in answer to the prayers of many."

—2 Corinthians 1:10b-11

Going Further and Deeper

Still More Strategies

The strategies explained earlier are most important, so please focus on them first. If you have already implemented most of them, or if any of these additional strategies seems valuable for your situation, they're available here to enhance your family's or ministry's prayer life.

M. Pray regularly with your peers. There's a camaraderie between fellow parents and ministry leaders that isn't available between leader and follower. If for no other reason, meet with peers in order to support others, and you'll find yourself receiving unexpected blessing.

N. Focus special training and encouragement toward those who are especially "given" to prayer. There are a variety of reasons such people may have an interest in prayer (see, for example, Luke 2:36-37). In order to encourage this strategic use of their time and energy, you may even have to encourage them to give up other ministry responsibilities. The payoff is well worth the sacrifice.

O. Plan and promote special prayer events, perhaps annually, as with a day or a week of prayer for unbelievers leading up to Easter—or at other intervals. Our church recently took the Islamic holy month of Ramadan to learn and practice how to pray for Muslims.

16. Acts 1:13-14 describes the beginning of a ten-day prayer event leading up to the amazing events of Pentecost, recorded in Acts 2. Consider how a special prayer event might become the occasion for something miraculous in your situation. Write down an idea or two.

P. Teach your people how to pray for the salvation of specific friends and family members. If our church's experience is any indicator, praying for lost friends and family will, more than any other topic, motivate people to gather for prayer. For specifics on how to pray for unbelievers, see Lesson 6.

17. How might you motivate those under your care to cultivate the same passion for the lost that Paul expressed in Romans 10:1?

Q. Expand your people's vision to include the world. Go out of your way to make your people's experience of the global need as real and as personal as possible; you will see a radical increase in their prayer fervency. Visit other cultures, invite multicultural guests and missionaries, or maintain correspondence with people around the world. This will bridge the gap between you and the world "out there," enabling you to experience the hearts and souls of people around the globe.

18. How can you, in your situation, help the people under your care to cultivate a passion for people worldwide, in keeping with Christ's commission to us (Acts 1:8)?

R. Expose your people to specially invited guests who can bring a new dimension to your prayer experience. These need not be experts—simply other learners who can shed fresh light on prayer.

S. Develop an effective way to receive prayer requests from your people and to distribute them to specific intercessors within the family or ministry. I recommend that requests always be written, even in a family or small group. Written requests are harder to forget. When people know they are being prayed for, they are more likely to pray themselves.

T. Where appropriate, focus your motivational efforts on men. For some reason unknown to me, the most fervent prayer warriors in most churches are women. By all means, do whatever you can to encourage them. At the same time, if the men in a family or ministry become devoted to prayer, others are more likely to follow.

U. Encourage faithful prayer for and with other families or ministries. By this means you can build the sense of unity and enthusiasm throughout the broader believing community, boosting each other's morale.

ETIQUETTE FOR PRAYING WITH OTHERS

∽◎∽

"The fewer the words the better the prayer."

—Martin Luther, Reformation leader (1483-1546)

Since this lesson draws largely from my practical experience, and contains less Scripture study than other lessons, consider spending extra time meditating on and memorizing Paul's prayer (the Memory Passage) near the end of the lesson. This prayer is an excellent model as you pray for yourself and other people.

"Mother, May I?"

Being the parents of eight very normal children, Patty and I are well acquainted with the perils of public family appearances. We are fairly intelligent, so it didn't take many embarrassing episodes for us to conclude that children aren't born with built-in manners. They must be taught. So we set about educating our kids on the finer points of "please," "thank you," and "excuse me." Due to our diligence, we can be reasonably confident that our children won't fall on their proverbial faces at a potluck.

Healthy and appropriate conduct in a corporate prayer meeting is also a skill that must be taught and learned, even for adults.

Growing up, I experienced more than my share of traditional prayer meetings—"traditional" in a negative sense. Most of these meetings were boring and irrelevant to me. The typical prayer meeting . . .

  . . . was uninspiring,

  . . . left most "participants" on the sidelines (if there were many to start with),

  . . . intimidated new believers and those who weren't verbally skilled,

  . . . was a non-event for the hard of hearing (as well as many whose hearing was just fine),

  . . . consisted of a jumble of unrelated requests and thoughts,

  . . . provided a handy platform for "preaching" or gossip in the guise of prayer, and

  . . . furnished a perfect haven of rest for the sleep deprived.

If most people's experience has been like mine was, it's no wonder so many prayer meetings are so poorly attended.

Simple Steps to Powerful Prayer

Prayer can be hard work, but corporate prayer need not be boring. At our church, we've devised a simple "prayer etiquette." This etiquette has added new vitality, interest, and energy to our prayer gatherings.

If you observe basic prayer etiquette, in time word will get around that your prayer gatherings are powerful and alive, producing real spiritual accomplishment. Violate these guidelines, and your prayer meetings will dwindle to a stubborn remnant with little spiritual impact.

Leaders should take time to explain prayer etiquette and implement a plan for frequent, nonthreatening reminders. People respond well if reminded of a guideline before they have a chance to violate it, rather than after they have committed an embarrassing blunder. If you are not in a leadership position, try tactfully presenting these guidelines to a leader, and let him or her do the teaching. In all circumstances, let your own example demonstrate basic prayer etiquette.

Basic Principles

A. Pray short prayers. When I was growing up, typically one person would stand and spend most of the meeting praying for all the missionaries. We all thought, *What devotion!* Then a couple others would fill out the remainder of the time. We couldn't understand why we never wanted to come back.

Why short prayers? It's difficult for most of us to stay attentive to one person praying for very long without becoming distracted and restless, especially if the prayer is not about us or an issue close to our hearts. This is just human nature. We can muster the attention needed to listen to and agree with a short prayer, but a meeting filled with long prayers will discourage people from returning.

Also, short prayers show courtesy toward younger believers. A recent survey shows that most people's greatest fear is that of public speaking. It's difficult enough for a new person to speak one sentence in front of others. They find a long prayer full of "churchy" language a hard act to follow, and they may never return. This may also give them a lifelong fear of praying out loud.

The short prayer rule is the most important to remind people about. Say it over and over (and over!), in humorous and varied ways, every time a group gets ready to pray.

What is a short prayer? The more people, the shorter the prayers. If there are only two, pray as long as you want. If you have six to twelve people, give a two-minute maximum—one minute is even better.

1. There is certainly a place for lengthy prayers, especially in private. But God also enjoys the shortest and simplest of prayers. What did God do in response to each of these short prayers?

Joshua 10:12-14

Judges 16:28-30

1 Kings 18:36-39

2 Kings 6:15-20

Matthew 9:27-29

John 11:41-45

See also Genesis 24:11-27, 28:1, 3-4; Numbers 12:13,15; 2 Samuel 15:31, 17:14, 23; Isaiah 6:8; Jonah 1:14-16; Matthew 8:24-27; Luke 11:2-4.

Practical Exercise: *Either by yourself or in a group, take time to pray a few short prayers. One sentence is often adequate. Keep each prayer under a minute. Time yourself; some of us lose track of time and need to experience what a shorter prayer feels like. Remember, these are real prayers. Think about the One who is listening.*

B. Pray loud enough for all to hear. Try an experiment. A few minutes into a prayer meeting ask yourself, "How much energy is in this room?" Then ask everyone to increase their volume twenty-five percent. You will be amazed how this one simple adjustment changes the corporate energy! When people pray more loudly, they pray faster and with greater emotional fervency.

Some may object, "Louder? I'm praying to God, not to you." I answer, "This is corporate prayer. You can talk privately with God at home. In this meeting I want to be able to agree with your prayer, so I need to hear you." Many people mistakenly equate reverence with quietness. Encourage people to lift their heads, rather than talking to the floor. An energetic group will keep people alert and involved.

2. In Acts 1:14 and 4:24, people were able to agree with each other in large corporate settings . . . all without a PA system! Describe the energy implicit in each passage.

Practical Exercise: *Either by yourself or in a group, try praying quietly for a short* *time, then pray a few decibels louder. Pray long enough that you get past self-consciousness about your volume. Write down your observations regarding your own experience and, if you're in a group, what you notice about the prayers of others.*

C. Don't go to sleep. For many, this can actually require discipline.

I grew up rising early to milk the cows, catching the school bus, attending basketball practice, returning home for more chores, then doing homework before hitting the sack. I learned to sleep instantly whenever possible. On the bus or during quiet moments in class, I could be asleep in thirty seconds. I still possess this singular talent. Once when I was newly married, my wife said, "You keep your eyes open when we kiss." "Yeah," I foolishly replied, "if I close them I'll go to sleep."

Now, if I can't stay awake while kissing my wife, I certainly can't afford to close my eyes in prayer. I routinely pray with eyes open, often standing as well. Do whatever it takes without creating a distraction.

D. Work hard at agreeing. Don't drift mentally. I encourage people to respond verbally to others' prayers. Agreeing aloud keeps my attention on the other person's words and affirms him or her, just as in any other conversation. If these responses distract you, I'd encourage you to bear with them for a while, and see if you don't come to appreciate them.

Practical Exercise: *Take time to pray with eyes open, while standing or doing some activity that doesn't distract from prayer (walking, jogging, bike riding). In a group, reinforce your support for the prayer of another person verbally with a simple "Amen" (meaning, "I agree; let it be so"), "Yes" or even "Uh huh."*

E. Stay on one topic at a time. Have you ever tried to conduct a conversation with one of those people who changes topics seven times in five minutes? You finally just smile and nod, because you've lost the train of thought. In prayer, as in any conversation, people are able to track with each other if the flow has consistency and avoids frequent, sudden topic changes. Spend several minutes on a single topic before moving on.

F. Try to connect with the person who prayed before you. In any prayer gathering, topic changes are necessary. But think of prayer as a conversation with some type of connection from topic to topic. Sudden shifts to unrelated topics cause mental whiplash and fatigue. Connected prayer fosters agreement and unity. Begin your prayer by agreeing with the previous prayer, and then add something related to the topic.

Practical Exercise: Next time you pray with others, make an effort to have at least three people in a row pray on a single topic before moving to something else. When you switch topics, try to choose a new topic that somehow flows out of the preceding one. Afterward, talk together about the experience. How did the continuity affect your ability to stay attentive to what others were praying about?

G. Listen to your thoughts. For some reason, corporate prayer is the setting where I do my most effective listening to God and my thoughts. I take notes, asking God to direct my prayer and to make known His will for the group. Then I pray for those matters I discern to be His will.

There are four possible sources of thoughts that come to our minds.

- Self. Each of us has our own original thoughts.
- The world around us. This includes both good influences (as when my wife's helpful reminders come to mind) and bad (as when TV ads cause me to think I need something I don't).
- The devil. Satan talks to us, just as he did to Jesus (Matthew 4:1-11).
- God.

Here's the problem: Those thoughts aren't accented to help us distinguish between the different sources. How can we sort out the "voices" and learn to zero in on the ones we want to hear?

3. Read John 10:1-5. According to Jesus, the sheep recognize the Shepherd's voice because they have gotten to know Him. What kinds of habits in your life will help you know God better, so you can learn to distinguish His guidance from that of other sources?

If my thoughts cause fearfulness they are not from God because He promises not to give a spirit of fear but of love and a sound mind

H. Bring a notebook and write down ideas, thoughts, and prayers. Writing helps some people keep their brain engaged in prayer. Thoughts that come to mind during prayer may provide direction for my life, and I need to keep track of them. For those who fear praying out loud, there's nothing wrong with praying by reading something you've written.

Practical Exercise: *Find or buy a notebook for prayer notes. Keep it with you during both private and corporate prayer. Write down at least three thoughts that cross your mind during each prayer session, and at some later time talk further with God about the value of what you have written. Are there goals to achieve? People to minister to? Helpful insights? What else of value do you find in your notes?*

I. Pray silently as long as necessary, but press on to become a vocal participant. The more you pray aloud, the more you will feel like an active participant. Others will benefit, sharing in your unique conversation with God. They'll get to agree with your requests, and they may be challenged and encouraged by your example and passion.

Practical Exercise: *If you are at all afraid of praying aloud with others, stop now and write a one-sentence prayer you want to use next time you pray with a group. Keep it simple and to the point, and God will hear you just as clearly as the person with the fifty-cent words. If you have trouble coming up with an idea, consider putting one thought from the following Scripture prayers into your own words: Psalms 23, 27, 139; Luke 11:2-4; Ephesians 1:15-19, 3:14-21; Colossians 1:9-12.*

It's Not Mechanical

"But, Dee," you might be saying, "this sounds so mechanical. This can't possibly be the way to pray with authenticity and true spirituality, can it?" I understand this objection, and I can identify with it. Sometimes when I'm learning a new skill, the basic techniques and guidelines can take over my focus for a time, until they become second nature, and I can focus on the main task.

Prayer is a skill, and, as with any new skill, it takes practice and guidance. You never see a tackle dummy, a blocking sled or a row of tires in the middle of a football game. Yet the players spend hours becoming intimately acquainted with this equipment most days of the season. The equipment helps them perfect their technique until fundamentals become second nature, so they can enjoy and excel at the main event.

These guidelines give participants confidence that they will enjoy the prayers of others and that they themselves will be valuable contributors. Howard Hendricks says that one of the best ways to motivate people is to show them how. Prayer etiquette provides the how-tos of corporate prayer, and we've seen people skyrocket in their enthusiasm for and enjoyment of group prayer as a result.

The Next Step
Continue to the next step in "Twenty Steps to Daily Prayer" (page 147).

Memory Passage
> "For this reason, since the day we heard about you, we have not stopped praying for you and asking God to fill you with the knowledge of his will through all spiritual wisdom and understanding. And we pray this in order that you may live a life worthy of the Lord and may please him in every way: bearing fruit in every good work, growing in the knowledge of God, being strengthened with all power according to his glorious might so that you may have great endurance and patience, joyfully giving thanks to the Father, who has qualified you to share in the inheritance of the saints in the kingdom of light."
>
> —Colossians 1:9-12

Going Further and Deeper

Here are several more practical pointers that apply to private and corporate prayer. These tend to be more applicable to specific situations or specific types of problems.

J. Don't pray private prayer needs in larger groups. Here I'm referring to settings of twenty or more people, where some people don't know each other. Larger groups should focus on concerns that are common to the church or to that group. Your mother's arthritic knee is important to you, but don't raise this request with people who don't know her or you.

In more intimate groups, such as families or cell groups, these personal concerns are part of the reason for the group's existence and should certainly be raised. These are people who are purposefully wanting to learn what is going on in each other's lives.

K. Don't gossip or slander as you pray. As a rule, I instruct my church to avoid individual names in large meetings, where someone might be present who isn't within a circle of confidentiality.

L. Don't preach as you pray. Remember, God is the audience. A person who commits this offense seldom understands what they are doing. There's some burden on their heart or something they want others to hear, and they take advantage of the captive audience, bouncing their "prayers" off the ceiling. Warn people about this preventively, but be prepared to talk privately and tactfully with an offender after the fact.

Lesson 10

ACCOUNTABILITY THAT WORKS

∽◉∾

"By friendship you mean the greatest love, the greatest usefulness,

the most open communication, the noblest sufferings, the severest truth,

the heartiest counsel, and the greatest union of minds of which

brave men and women are capable."

—Jeremy Taylor, English prelate (1613-1667)

"Insomuch as any one pushes you nearer to God, he or she is your friend."

—Anonymous

Together We Can Do the Impossible

In a previous lesson I told you about the day my doctor said, "Lose weight or you will die." That kind of statement has a way of producing fresh motivation. Shortly thereafter, a friend invited me to join our church team in the Hood-to-Coast relay—a relay race from Mount Hood's 6000-foot level to the Oregon coast. In a moment of insanity, I agreed.

I began to run in a local gym, starting with one lap, at the end of which I sounded exactly like a wounded seal I had once seen at the coast. The next day I ran two laps. Soon I could run a mile. But I would not have gotten beyond that first torturous lap if not for a phone call that evening from my friend, and daily calls thereafter. Because of his loving commitment, I actually completed every inch of my part in the relay.

Later I participated in a marathon. Partway through the race, I was far behind my time goal, struggling up the incline of a long bridge. Near the top of the bridge sat a man in a lawn chair with a homemade sign that read, "You can do it." He saw me coming and called out, "Hey, number 342! I made this sign just for you!" I knew he hadn't, but I went on to beat my goal by two minutes.

The power of encouragement is amazing. Together we can achieve what we could never, in a million years, achieve alone—such as a sacrificial prayer life. Everyone knows we need accountability, but few people know how to use it effectively. Even when it's done poorly, an accountability relationship can be helpful simply because we were never designed to live life alone, especially the difficult parts.

Asking for and receiving help is humbling. Pride gets in the way—either that or laziness and fear of change. But without the loving support of an accountability partner, you will progress little in the spiritual disciplines. If you want to rise higher, to do what you've never found yourself able to do before, plan to invest time in the practices that bring blessing. You'll need others' help.

When I first started communicating my newfound passion for prayer in my church, I received little response. I couldn't comprehend why other people weren't as excited as I was. Then I started to implement the principle of loving accountability in my church. Gradually I saw the results I had hoped for. I was now able to move people in large numbers toward faithful, daily, persistent prayer.

An accountability partner or group is committed to helping you be your best and serves to remind you of the blessings to be gained if you persevere in prayer. Results can take time. But you need to understand the ingredients that make the difference between mere socializing and accountability that works.

Principles for Accountability

A. Sincerely acknowledge that you need accountability to remain faithful to the spiritual disciplines. If you don't think you need accountability, you won't contribute well to an accountability relationship. Few are able to be disciplined alone. Discipline requires encouragement.

1. From each of the following passages, describe the achievements to be reached and the dangers to be avoided through accountability.

Hebrews 3:12-13

1 Thessalonians 2:11-12

Titus 1:13

Stop and take a significant amount of time with God to consider your attitude toward accountability.

- Tell Him about your past experiences, whether enjoyable or disappointing.
- Talk about your inner humility or pride, and how hard or easy it is for you to be transparent with others and to receive honest feedback.
- Dream with Him about the blessing you want to enjoy through disciplined obedience, and what it will take for you to bear fruit in abundance.
- Ask Him to keep you open to His heart and mind throughout the rest of this lesson.

B. Remain faithful to the group. You reap what you sow (Galatians 6:7). As with any endeavor, you will benefit in direct proportion to your investment.

Basics of accountability group faithfulness:

- Commit to weekly reports. Even if you report failure, checking in cultivates trust, support and vital communication habits.
- Do not be satisfied with "close." Gradual progress by increments is good, but don't stop or plateau. Receive and give acceptance, love, and encouragement all along the way, but settle for nothing less than the goals you believe God has called you to pursue in His

strength and in the company of His people.

- Do your part to keep the group from mediocrity. The group, as a whole, tends toward the least committed person. Help hold others up.
- Remember that faithfulness, even in things we consider small, is a key to greater blessings from God.

2. Read the teachings of Jesus in Luke 16:10 and Matthew 25:21. Think of some examples where your faithfulness might lead to even greater opportunities in the future.

C. Positive habits and behaviors are the focus of accountability. Don't focus on sin and failure. Not only is this less effective motivation, but failure isn't measurable. If you focus positively on good habitual behaviors, you can measure your success, and you'll know when you're reaching your goals. You'll also find that, with a focus on right behavior, sins and failures take care of themselves.

3. From the following passages, summarize the kind of emphasis that leads to genuine growth and spiritual success: Joshua 1:8; Psalm 1:1-3; Matthew 6:33.

face your problems with
Gods Presence
Gods Power
Gods Promises

D. Faithful, fruitful living is the goal; accountability is only the method. You don't practice piano in order to practice, but to enjoy the fruit of playing well. Accountability is not the end, but the means to holy living.

Should you set goals and be accountable if you don't enjoy it? Sure, because it produces fruit. Frankly, spiritual disciplines can sometimes be dry as dirt. But it's not the disciplines that we get the charge out of. We're working toward spiritual fruit, changed lives, ministry impact, a growing relationship with God, joy and satisfaction from accomplishing something worthwhile. Lift your eyes and take the long view past the method to the goal—the kingdom of God ruling under every roof and in every heart, including yours.

4. Suppose a friend of yours read 1 Corinthians 9:24-27 and said, "Boy, is this guy legalistic, or what?" How would you respond?

5. In your own words, describe the fruit of spiritual discipline in each of these passages:

Colossians 2:5

1 Timothy 4:7-8

E. Encourage each other intelligently. Truly listen to one another. Try to choose methods of encouragement that are best suited to the individual and the situation; one size doesn't fit all. Some people are motivated by direct confrontation, some by compassionate partnership, and so on.

6. In Hebrews 10:24-25, the word "consider" means "study, examine, reflect on, think carefully." What does it take for a group to develop this kind of person-to-person understanding?

F. Rapid results can come only with humility. Humility essentially says, "I need other people; I can't do it on my own." Humility seeks out and accepts others' help. How do you respond when others correct or reprove you, especially when it's offered in love? If you will receive the difficult statements, you'll grow quickly.

7. Read Proverbs 9:8 and 29:1. Take a few minutes and talk to your Father about your attitude toward the guidance He offers for your good, through people or other avenues.

G. The accountability group works best if everyone focuses on the same goals. I've tried groups with individualized goals, but they haven't worked for me. Multiple goal lists are confusing and hard to track. I recommend that everyone be held to the same basic standards for weekly reporting, even if these are easy for some and hard for others. Different people will find different goals more challenging, and there tends to be an equalizing effect. Members may create additional, personalized goals to be discussed less frequently.

H. The group disciplines or goals need to be few and basic. Too many goals confuse the group, hurting effectiveness. My groups never go beyond a dozen goals, including "Don't blow smoke" (don't lie about the other goals), which is actually a rule of group conduct. It's amazing how the positive impact of a few basic disciplines spreads to every area of your life.

I. Emphasize personal communication and other appropriate relationship-building techniques. Deeper relationships and frequent communication are signs of an effective group. Group members need more contact that just submitting weekly reports, but little time need be invested in order to deepen relationships, especially with the advent of email. This way trust is accumulated and stored, eventually forming a safe, solid basis for intimate, life-changing impact between friends.

J. Share prayer requests, and pray for each other faithfully. I pray as I read my partners' reports. This is my most important ministry to them. I pray for strengthened discipline and increased passion. Prayer combined with accountability has proven to be a life-changing force.

K. Get a grip on any tendency to excuse and "blow smoke." No matter what our personalities, our strengths or our weaknesses, each of us stands responsible before God to decide the paths we will follow—leading to life or leading to destruction (Deuteronomy 30:19), or worse, to lukewarm complacency. Each of us will discover, in Christ, all we need in order to obey God and find life. Temperament or gifting is never an excuse for lack of discipline or poor time stewardship.

God has proven to me that our weaknesses do not excuse disobedience. I'm not naturally a people person. Is that an excuse for me to go through life offending people? No. I've learned to compensate in order to be obedient and effective in my relationships. God has supernaturally granted me all I've needed in order to be a faithful steward of people.

8. How does Moses' end-of-life challenge to Israel (Deuteronomy 30:15-20) speak to you in your life situation today?

9. What are the differences between the wise and the unwise, according to Ephesians 5:15-16?

L. Everything rises and falls on leadership. The most common reason accountability groups fail is lack of leadership. The leader doesn't have to be smarter or even more mature, but someone must ask the tough questions, or the group's standards will slide, and real accountability will be lost. If you find yourself in a group without leadership, you don't have to label yourself a leader—just lead. Take the initiative, guide the group in setting the ground rules, live by them as an example, and ask how commitments are progressing. Those who take it seriously will taste the rich fruit of healthy accountability and will begin either to support your leadership or to share in the responsibility themselves.

10. Look back at Principle A. Talk to your Father about how you truly think and feel about accountability. If you come to the conclusion that it's worth your while, then continue to 11.

11. If you are not currently involved in an accountability group or partnership, take a few days to pray about the people you might invite to partner with you—perhaps people who will benefit you, or people in whom you can invest, or, preferably, both. Then share the principles of this lesson with them, and start planning together.

12. If you are currently involved in an accountability group, go back through this lesson and check off the principles your group is already using. Then pray over which one or two new principles would be most important for your group to implement, in order to improve your effectiveness. Pray about the best way to present these suggested improvements to your accountability partners.

One More Story

Growing up, the activity I enjoyed above all else was fishing with my dad. Dad would never fish alone; he always took at least one of us boys. Every time we left the house, he would say, "Fishing is something you do with someone you care about." Later, sitting by the water, I'd ask why it was so important to fish in company. Dad would say, "Some things bring so much joy you want to do them with someone else. When I catch my fish, I want to show it to someone who matters to me."

Some things are meant to be done together. I believe one is prayer, supported by accountability. Throughout the Bible, people prayed together as the norm, not the exception. Together, we can stimulate each other on to greater heights with God than we could ever reach alone.

The Next Step

How's your prayer habit coming along? Is someone helping you? Are you helping someone else? Turn to "Twenty Steps to Daily Prayer" (page 147) and take the next step.

Memory Passage

"Train yourself to be godly. For physical training is of some value, but godliness has value for all things, holding promise for both the present life and the life to come."

—1 Timothy 4:7b-8

Going Further and Deeper

M. Accountability groups are not primarily support groups. We all hurt and have bad days. But focus your accountability discussions on the positive direction you want to go. Feel free to share briefly your disappointments and difficulties for prayer support, but don't belabor them. Focus on the good things that can happen when you faithfully live the disciplines and experience God's blessing in your lives.

N. Accountability is incomplete without reproof and correction. This is where many accountability groups fail. They form a good-old-boy club with unspoken mutual agreements, "I won't ask you the hard questions if you won't ask me."

13. How can reproof and correction be done constructively, rather than destructively (Proverbs 27:6; Psalm 141:5; 1 Timothy 5:20)?

O. Do not use the "legalism" cop-out. We should be able to distinguish legalism from healthy standards, faithful commitments and diligent self-evaluation. Willingness to applying these challenging aspects of holy living is wisdom, pure and simple.

Every serious basketball player understands that when you're late for practice there is a consequence—you may not get to start or you may run extra laps. Life is full of responsibility and consequences. With any life skill, the person who practices the most will perform the best. Discipline and accountability keep us practicing healthy, holy living.

Even those who are talented won't fulfill the potential of their giftedness without practice. Let's not forget this principle when it comes to the most important skills of all—the skills of living righteously in a world where God reigns over all with absolute power, perfect wisdom and steadfast love.

A note to those who resist time management: Stewarding our limited time, in order to accomplish only God's best, is a good thing, not legalism. It shows that you value God. If time management is hard for you, that's understandable. God will enable you to do the supernatural—to use wisely what He has entrusted to you, that you might rise above mediocrity into abundant life. He will do this if you rely on His strength and the support of other believers.

GROWTH THROUGH GOALS

∾ৎ৶৹

"Everything we say or do is moving toward a goal. As people we are teleological beings; that is, we are controlled by our goals. If we want to change what we are doing, then we must first change what we are trying to accomplish."

—Larry Crabb, psychologist

"Goal setting is an attempt to uncover God's strategy and will, and become part of it."

—Ed Dayton

Steady as She Goes

When I was a kid, Dad took us on an aircraft carrier. Down in the bottom were three huge gyroscopes, many tons each, as big as houses. Dad explained that, in rough seas, jets would normally be unable to take off and land on the moving deck. Under those conditions, the crew would start the gyroscopes spinning, like tops or bike wheels. Amazingly, the gyros would then hold that city-sized carrier steady even in high seas, so the jets could operate safely.

Our lives are like that carrier. Our steadiness, our faithfulness to keep on living well, can be rocked by circumstances and other influences. Choosing and reviewing God-honoring goals sets up a gyroscope-like force in our hearts, that serves to steady our lives, to help us maintain course and deal rightly with circumstances. By writing our goals and then reading and praying through them repeatedly, even just twice a week, we give the Holy Spirit a tool to strengthen our focus and our determination to pursue the course God has set for us.

Now, I understand that some people like goals better than others do. God has created us differently (Lesson 5). But there are some life skills that no believer can effectively develop without setting goals, so these principles apply to everyone. If you love goals, then let these principles make a good thing better. If you despise goals, then consider the value of and scriptural support for what I share. Then decide whether goals might help you seek God and His values.

Goals in Two Easy Steps

I have a simple two-part concept of goals that I think will comfort the skeptic. First, goal setting is simply putting your intentions in writing. I don't see goals as shackles to hold you down, but rather as reminders to help you see more clearly the direction you and God agreed was good for your life. It is important to seek God through prayer as you work on your goals. That way, we aren't just coming up with things we want for our lives, but rather, we are listening for what God's goals for us are.

Some are critical of goal setting. They point to James 4:13-15 as proof against goal setting:

> "Now listen, you people who say, 'Today or tomorrow we will go to this or that city, spend a year there, carry on business and make money.' Why, you do not even know what will happen tomorrow. What is your life? You are a mist that appears for a little while and then vanishes. Instead, you ought to say, 'If it is the Lord's will, we will live and do this or that.'"

These verses *seem* to be against goal setting. I think they are talking about acting upon haphazard decisions. You're not rewriting the Ten Commandments; you're simply putting your own desires—based on your time seeking God—in writing, and they can be revised whenever and however you see fit.

Second, allow your goals to have their ongoing influence simply by reading them regularly. Many powerful and well-intentioned goals never achieve their purpose, because they are written, then forgotten. Write your goals where you will read them at least once or twice a week. As you are repeatedly exposed to those dreams and plans, just watch where God and your heart take you—places you wouldn't have gone without frequent reminders of your dreams.

The seven principles presented in this lesson are descriptions of what goals are, rather than explanations of how to set and keep goals. In the preceding two paragraphs I've already told you all you need to know about setting goals: (1) write down your desires, and (2) read what you've written, over and over. What is lacking in many people's thinking is not the how, but the why. So consider my definitions of goals throughout this lesson, and allow them to challenge your own assumptions about how you grow and relate to God.

What Is a Goal? (Seven Answers)

A. Goal setting is functioning as we were designed to function best, because we've been created in the image and likeness of God. We, like God, have the capacity to think toward the future. I believe God intends each of us to maximize our potential by using this capacity to discover God's will and to determine to follow it. We find security in the fact that God has established His plans long in advance, and that He never fails to do exactly what He has intended from the start. When we follow His example, making plans and taking steps to fulfill them, we live more secure and fruitful lives.

1. According to Genesis 1:27, "God created man in his own image, in the image of God he created him; male and female he created them." Read the following passages, and list the words and phrases that show God planning toward the future.

Psalm 33:11

Isaiah 14:24-27

Isaiah 25:1

Isaiah 46:9-11

Isaiah 55:11

Jeremiah 29:11-13

Matthew 16:21

Objection #1: Goal setting is worldly.

Response: People didn't invent goal setting; they discovered it. It is a universal tool provided by God that the world uses well and the church has ignored. The world uses goals to make money; the church must learn to use goals to make disciples. Goal setting makes us choose priorities and think carefully about what is truly important.

2. Now read the following passages and list the words and phrases that show God's intention that humans follow His example of planning toward the future.

Proverbs 21:5

Isaiah 32:8

Proverbs 16:3

Lamentations 1:9

1 Corinthians 9:24-27

2 Corinthians 9:5,7

A man once called inviting me to consider leaving Jefferson Baptist Church to take another ministry position. Without hesitation, I thanked him for the honor, but I declined. He asked, "Aren't you going to pray about it?" I answered, "I already have—not about this specific invitation, but about staying here in Jefferson. In fact, I've determined that it's God's will that I die here." He was stunned. "How can you know what God wants you to do five years down the road?" he asked. I responded then, and still say, "Why can't I? Where is it written that God only reveals His will five minutes ahead of time?"

In fact, Scripture makes it abundantly clear that God does not act impulsively, and He doesn't expect us to either. God has planned all of history, and He has revealed much of His will centuries in advance. He follows much the same pattern in personal and ministry guidance. One reason we may avoid seeking God's will far in advance is that it requires diligent prayer. If we discover His will for the next five years, pursuing it requires steadfast persistence. It isn't easy.

B. Goal setting is premeditated decision making, just as when you make a budget or establish standards for your kids to live by.

3. In Luke 14:28-32, Jesus teaches planning ahead as common sense. List three areas in which you could not function without planning.

Objection #2: Goal setting is fleshly and quenches the Holy Spirit's leading and guiding in our lives (James 4:13-16).

Response: Actually, those who seek the Holy Spirit's guidance, before the pressure of the decision deadline, are much more apt to be within God's will than those who wait and often decide impulsively. James is not saying that planning is wrong, but that leaving God out of the plans is wrong.

4. Many people take Proverbs 16:9 to imply that planning is wrong. Read this verse as though the first part and the second part are parallel, speaking of two things that happen at the same time. How would you now summarize this verse in your own words?

C. Goal setting is attempting to steward well the authority God has entrusted to us, in order to advance His kingdom. The key word is "steward." We find fulfillment when we manage faithfully what God has entrusted to us. Among other things, He grants us each a degree of authority, sovereignty, influence, control. If I steward that sovereignty well, He will entrust more to me. We can accomplish nothing without God's authority. The more authority we receive from God, the more we can accomplish for His kingdom, to the point that God will use us far beyond anyone's expectations. It all starts with prayer and our faithfulness with what we've been given; such faithfulness requires careful forethought.

5. According to each of these passages, what kind of conduct does God reward with increased authority?

Daniel 4:30-32

Matthew 25:21,23,29

Objection #3: Goal setting encourages independence from God and pride in our own accomplishments.

Response: Goal setting is a morally neutral tool that can be applied pridefully or humbly. Our heart attitude determines whether we pursue our own goals or God's. If we use goal setting as wise stewards, we will be reminded, every time we set or accomplish a goal, that we do so by the authority that is ours in the name of Jesus. Goal setting can thus move us toward humility and gratitude.

D. A goal is a statement of repentant intention, based on conviction, to change our conduct. "Repent" means to "change your mind," implying also an outward change of behavior. John the Baptist, Jesus and the Apostles basically preached, "Repent." The appropriate response is, "Okay, I will." Goals are decisions to change our behavior.

6. Read Jesus' words in Revelation 2:4-5. Describe one unfulfilled intention you would like to revisit with fresh commitment.

E. A goal is a statement of commitment to obey God. Each of us has experienced the frustration of a besetting sin—a bad habit that we wish we could stop, but to which we keep returning. I've seen individuals make amazing breakthroughs to obedience by these simple steps: (1) examining and measuring what they are currently doing, (2) writing down a measurable target behavior, (3) praying for God's help, (4) inviting another person's support through accountability and (5) regularly rereading the goal. Taking the desire from your mind and writing it down in clear terms can make all the difference.

7. Moses reduced all of life down to one decision (Deuteronomy 30:19-20). What form might this decision take for you?

F. A goal is a statement of faith concerning what we believe God wants to do through us in the future. We must hold these goals loosely so we can revise them as we gain new insights into God's will. We become more adept at understanding God's will as we mature, getting to know Him better, beginning to think and feel more as He does.

8. How does faith relate to the fulfillment of God-honoring goals (Hebrews 11:1,6; Matthew 15:28, 17:20)?

G. A goal is a statement of a dream we believe God has given us. Those who pray a lot dream a lot. A few years ago in Thailand, while standing and praying on a mountaintop overlooking Bangkok, I began to dream of learning Thai and returning for a short time to plant a church in Bangkok. God has fulfilled that dream in His own way. We now support a Thai pastor who has planted one church and will soon plant a second.

A goal is a written description of a dream. Dreams are exciting, but they are hard to remember, so write them down, right away! Then you'll have them in more objective form, where you can fill them out, adjust them, receive counsel about them and hold onto them until they emerge from your imagination into reality.

9. Imagine yourself in the place of the men in Matthew 20:30-34. What if Jesus walked by you right now, stopped and asked, "What do you want me to do for you?" How would you answer?

10. What is God's attitude toward your honorable dreams (Psalms 20:4, 21:2, 37:4-5, 145:19)?

11. Read Proverbs 13:12,19a. Your very psychological and spiritual makeup is designed around dreams. In what specific ways might your Father desire to delight your heart?

Those who dream the most also pray the most and do the most. Those who see the invisible do the impossible. Despite what they say, the reason most people don't set measurable goals is fear of failure and of the pain of disappointment. Some live in a rut and call it faithfulness. But in Jesus' parable (Matthew 25:14-30), it was the servants who took risks of obedience and multiplied their talents who were called faithful. The one who played it safe out of fear was called wicked and lazy.

Here's the hard reality: Disappointment is painful. The greater the dream, the greater the disappointment if it isn't realized. Many believers, in an attempt to avoid pain, have effectively eliminated almost all hope, desire, and dreams from their life. There is a certain security in this, but these feeble souls rarely attract anyone to their faith.

> "It is not the critic who counts, not the man who points out how the strong man stumbled, or where the doer of deeds could have done them better. The credit belongs to the man who is actually in the arena; whose face is marred by dust and sweat and blood; who strives valiantly; who errs and comes short again and again; who knows the great enthusiasms, the great devotions, and spends himself in a worthy cause; who, at best, knows in the end the triumph of high achievement; and who, at the worst, if he fails, at least fails while daring greatly, so that his place shall never be with those cold and timid souls who know neither victory nor defeat."
>
> —Theodore Roosevelt

The Next Step
You've come a long way! Turn to "Twenty Steps to Daily Prayer" (page 147) and take your next step of prayer growth.

Memory Passage

"But the noble man makes noble plans, and by noble deeds he stands."

—Isaiah 32:8

Going Further and Deeper

Additional thoughts on Principle B: Individually, we need to set goals for our lives. Corporately we need to set goals for our ministries and programs. In this way the Holy Spirit can much more effectively move through our hearts and minds to direct before we act. Why do we think it is more spiritual to be controlled by the Spirit while we act, than to have our hearts, minds, and wills led by the Spirit before we act? Much impulsive decision making is actually unwise reaction to pressure; much of life's pressure would be avoided by more prayer and careful planning.

Additional thoughts on Principle C: We sometimes fail at stewardship because we forget to think in terms of God's timetable. God does not call in His accounts every week, or we would remain much more mindful of our role as stewards. In His wisdom, He has chosen to call in His accounts much farther down the road, requiring us to seek His will for longer-term planning.

> "Goals are an offering before the Lord. It is our way of saying, 'Lord, this is what we believe you want us to do, and this is what we intend to do. If you would like to direct us in another path, we are open to your leading. Meanwhile we move ahead in faith.'"
>
> —Ted Engstrom

As you step out and seek God for goals and the path to fulfilling the dreams He has given you, set a prayer plan in place. This will help you be systematic about praying for these goals, and it will allow the Holy Spirit more freedom in refining their fulfillment in you.

Lesson 12

PRAYER AND LEADERSHIP

⤳⧉⤲

"Be a pattern to others, and then all will go well: for as a whole city is affected by the licentious passions of great men, so it is likewise reformed by their moderation."

—Cicero, Roman statesman (106-43 BC)

"You do not lead by hitting people over the head—that's assault, not leadership."

—Dwight D. Eisenhower, 34th U.S. president (1890-1969)

"You've got to give loyalty down, if you want loyalty up."

—Donald T. Regan, U.S. secretary of the treasury 1981-1985

Authority Gained Is Authority Earned

I had to ask him to repeat himself. "You're in charge of the farm, Son." Dad looked me in the eye. "You're the oldest, and you're in high school now, practically a man. Your mother and I think you're ready for a man's responsibility. The cows, the dairy, it's all in your hands. We'll be back from the reunion in a week. Okay?"

"Okay!" What an opportunity! I was totally in charge. I could do whatever I wanted—for a week!

Dad left me a list of jobs that had to be completed. No problem. As soon as Dad and Mom were gone, I started on the list. But then it dawned on me that this was my chance to do some things I couldn't do with my parents around. And Dad's job list would still be there tomorrow. . . .

In the end, I completed fewer than half the jobs. To make matters worse, Dad and Mom returned two days early. I remember the sick feeling in my gut as I spotted the car turning into the driveway. Dad climbed out of the car, shook my hand and asked how things had gone. He glanced around; disappointment clouded his face. He didn't say anything then, but that evening he and I went for a walk. I've never forgotten his words: "You don't get responsibility just because you reach a certain age. It's always earned. If you act responsibly, you're given more authority and freedom. Because of your irresponsible behavior, the next time I have to leave, I'll be putting your brother in charge."

Those words cut me right through to my core. I determined then that I would never again behave irresponsibly.

I learned then that authority . . . responsibility . . . freedom . . . are always earned. That lesson has served me well through my ministry years, because God also grants greater authority based on how we've handled previous responsibility.

The Leader's Prayer Life

Prayer and effective leadership go hand in hand. Good leadership in prayer will result in followers who are growing in their prayer lives; poor leadership won't. If you want your people to thrive in their commitment to prayer, then you must provide a model they can respectfully follow, earning their respect by your example—never demanding it.

Any authority we possess is authority earned from our followers and from God. God is more likely to give authority to a man or woman who prays, who continually looks to Him for strength and vision. He trusts this leader to use His authority wisely.

By living compassionately, by modeling integrity, and by persistently seeking God through fervent prayer, good leaders establish a large equity of trust that allows them to make bigger mistakes than those with little or no equity. The leader who has lost authority, or who has not yet had time to earn authority, is wise at first to refrain from making great demands on his followers. Consistent, prayerful investment in your trust account will, in time, earn you the authority that you need for effective leadership.

1. What does God say about the types of authority He delegates and the types of people to whom He entrusts authority?

1 Chronicles 29:11-12

Daniel 5:18-20

Matthew 10:1

John 19:10-11

2 Corinthians 13:10

> "Successful leadership depends far more on the follower's perception of the leader than upon the leader's abilities. Leadership is in the eye of the follower."
> —James Kouzes and Barry Posner

Seven Character Qualities that Earn Authority

Most of us, when we pray, focus on concrete physical things. But one of the major areas of prayer emphasis in the Bible is praying for spiritual growth and character qualities—fruits of the Spirit. Jesus told Peter that he was praying that Peter would have the ability to withstand the attack of Satan (Luke 22:31). The Epistles record more than twenty of Paul's prayers for those in his charge. None of them mention any concrete physical request. All are for character traits that bring people into a deeper relationship with God. We need to be praying those things into our lives and the lives of those we pray for.

Here are some biblical qualities to pray into your own life and the lives of others:

A. Pray for faithfulness. A faithful leader is one who lives his life on the basis of convictions and commitments, not on the basis of circumstances and convenience. A faithful man or woman makes and keeps commitments—including and especially the commitment to prayer.

Pray that your disciplined lifestyle will give security and comfort to those under your care. People need leaders, and they want to follow, but they are reluctant to follow leaders who make them nervous. Be patient; keep living faithfully, and the trust will come.

In your requests for faithfulness, it is healthy to be a "wholist." Pray for faithfulness and commitment across the spectrum of life—physically, spiritually, intellectually, emotionally, socially.

2. Consider the security you feel as a result of God's faithfulness (Deuteronomy 7:9). How does this help you understand your followers' need for your faithfulness?

3. How might each of these passages help you shape your prayers for faithfulness?

Matthew 24:45-47, 25:21

1 Samuel 2:35

1 Corinthians 4:1-2

1 Timothy 1:12

2 Timothy 2:2

B. Pray for a servant's heart. A servant's heart is measured best by the way we respond to tough relational issues between ourselves and those under our care. When Jesus uses the term "servant," it is commonly misinterpreted to mean the one who is called on whenever the toilet becomes clogged, doing the kinds of things a servant does. In reality, Jesus usually used the term in the context of conflict to describe a relational attitude. God can help you follow Jesus' example, serving others by responding to conflict in a healthy, godly manner.

Pray that you might not become easily offended, and that you might avoid offending others. When conflict does arise, ask God to fill you with forgiveness and acceptance, rather than defensiveness and retaliation. A defensive leader will be ineffective, receiving little or no authority from God.

A leader must learn to give his or her life away to people, even when those people respond with slights and insults. Ask for eyes to see the offenders as Jesus told us to view our enemies, returning blessings for curses. Pray for initiative as a peacemaker, to see each conflict through to true resolution.

Please understand, serving does not mean giving away your leadership. There is a big difference between lording it over people (an expression of fear) and exercising authority (an expression of secure, humble servanthood). Either extreme—lording or failing to lead—causes disunity and loss of respect. Ask God to help you find the healthy middle ground: leading without lording.

4. How, specifically, might you pray, in order to attain the heart and conduct of a servant leader?

Mark 10:42-45

not indignant because they disagree but rather be willing to serve them

Romans 14:19

ask God what you can do to restore peace and to build all involved up till all are edified.

Psalm 34:14

make sure your own heart is free of evil, then seek a peaceful solution, keep seeking it.

1 Peter 5:1-3

be willing to shepherd each one, be eager to do so.

C. Pray for love for people. If you accept God's help with loving especially those who are not lovely, you will do an excellent job with all the rest. Pray for your communication, that your followers might know their shepherd's voice and hear clearly a message of love.

With difficult people, God is trusting you with your greatest opportunities for growth and increased impact, because your dealings with these people provide the litmus test by which your leadership authority will be evaluated. Here is where your authority is either proven and matured . . . or diminished and lost. Authority is a loaded gun, and God won't give it to anyone who doesn't know how to use it in submission to Him.

5. *Read John 10:2-3,11-13. What can you ask God to help you do—and avoid—in order to follow Jesus' example as a good shepherd?*

(private conduct)

holiness is not so much actions as it is character

D. Pray for holiness—not just for holy actions, but for holy character, in keeping with the character of the God who lives within you (Ephesians 4:22-24). Seek to be guided by conviction of God's truth, not by the opinions of men (Matthew 15:1-20, 23:25-28).

Pray that your private life would be worthy of authority from God, because private conduct is the true measure of your trustworthiness. When temptation ambushes you, ask God for wisdom to find the escape hatch He promises, and pray for the power to walk through it, that you might maintain purity and holiness (1 Corinthians 10:13).

A key to holiness is healthy self-examination in God's presence, resulting in confession and repentance. There are two opposite errors to avoid here. On the one hand, beware of false guilt. Look inside for specific sin, and when you find it, confess it and receive cleansing. On the other hand, watch for superficiality and denial about your sin, which allow sin to grow to the point of self-destruction. The freedom and power that come through humble honesty and forgiveness are well worth the discomfort of confession. I've found journaling to be a helpful method of self-examination.

6. *Read the prayer in Psalm 139:23-24 slowly a few times. Stop to consider each phrase's meaning. Speak each phrase from your heart to God. He will honor this prayer coming from an honest heart.* *all scripture can be turned into a prayer*

If God's Spirit brings to mind specific sins you have done, then turn next to 1 John 1:7-9, and read it carefully. If it is your desire to be cleansed and forgiven, then mentally step into the light before God and confess (literally "agree about") your sin to Him. The instant you do this, God guarantees that you are completely cleansed of that sin. This passage implies that confession is an ongoing, repeated habit that we need to maintain as new sins come to light.

E. Pray for responsibility. Everything a leader does has an impact on everyone he is leading, even if no one recognizes it. The repercussions of the leader's conduct and character spread far and wide, and last through generations and centuries.

Pray that you might become more conscientious about your lifestyle. Ask God to sustain in you a holy fear that will keep you walking with Him, trusting with complete dependence on His strength, rather than your own. Ask Him to help you comprehend the magnitude of the stewardship He's entrusted to you.

7. There are lessons for all leaders in God's warning to teachers (James 3:1) and the story of David in 1 Chronicles 21:1-17. How will these passages affect your prayers for yourself and those in your care?

F. Pray for humility. For some leaders, praise from people can become as much a stumbling block as criticism. When God uses you as an instrument of righteousness to accomplish a great work, pray for an attitude that gives God glory.

8. What fruit could you bear, and what traps could you avoid, by praying for humility?

Daniel 5:20

1 Corinthians 4:7

James 4:6

G. Pray for careful handling of God's Word. If you have a role that involves formal Scripture teaching or even informal discussion of the Bible, your care in the way you interpret and apply Scripture can lead to significant victory in your people's lives. People who know that you, their leader, are solidly founded on the wisdom of God's Word will follow you anywhere.

9. How should you be praying for your handling and teaching of God's Word?

Malachi 2:6-9

2 Timothy 2:15

2 Timothy 4:2

The Next Step

If you've completed these lessons in order, then you may now be coming to the twelfth step or higher in "Twenty Steps to Daily Prayer" (page 147). Take time to thank and praise God for the progress you've made. Please also consider this experience as a launching pad for your continued development of your prayer life. God will always be there, looking forward to your visits with Him.

Memory Passage

"Jesus called them together and said, 'You know that those who are recognized as rulers of the Gentiles lord it over them, and their high officials exercise authority over them. Not so with you. Instead, whoever wants to become great among you must be your servant, and whoever wants to be first must be slave of all. For even the Son of Man did not come to be served, but to serve, and to give his life as a ransom for many.'"

—Mark 10:42-45

Going Further and Deeper

Six Major Killers of Faithfulness

While you are praying proactively for positive character qualities, pray also that God would protect you from the following dangers.

A. Lack of discipline in the "small" and "unimportant." At around age nine, my son Seth received a BB gun for Christmas. I don't like BB guns, because they teach kids to be careless with real ones. I had a talk with Seth, and said, "We're going to pretend that this gun is a 30.06 (rifle). If I see you violate any principles of gun safety, that gun is going in the dump. No second chances. The risks are too high."

We miss this principle in other areas of life where the consequences of negligence are not immediately obvious. We become lax in the seemingly small and unimportant, but the laxity carries over, perhaps in ways we don't even recognize, into more important areas of life.

10. How important are the "little things" according to Jesus in Luke 16:10? Which "little things" do you need to make a matter of consistent prayer?

B. Lack of discipline in the areas no one else knows about. Probably the most common violation of this principle is TV viewing. We spend our energy in good pursuits and then think, "I've earned some down time." Then we spend it absorbing whatever might come on during the next two hours. Even if no one on earth ever sees me involved in dangerous behavior, God sees, and He is the one who gives and takes away authority.

11. Use 2 Chronicles 16:9 to formulate a prayer for yourself, that your heart might become completely God's.

C. Neglecting to set personal goals and write them down. Putting your commitments in writing makes them tangible and demonstrates that you take them seriously. The pressures of life are stronger than your memory, and you will lose what you don't record.

D. Reluctance to be accountable to others for our goals. Many of us—especially us men—do not easily allow others into our lives. If you want to pursue your God-given goals, others can help us be accountable. Don't neglect this powerful truth.

12. How might Proverbs 27:17 help you pray for your attitudes and relationships? Why does the value of accountability outweigh the discomfort?

E. Defensiveness and denial when others react to the undisciplined areas of our lives. People may not even realize what they are reacting to, but they will behave differently toward a leader who is disciplined than they will toward one who is undisciplined. Do yourself and your followers the service of praying for a humble, attentive response to these types of reactions, that you might learn and grow from them.

F. Giving in to weariness and discouragement during tough times. Faithful leaders remain faithful by learning how to manage pressure. It's when you're most fatigued or stressed that you need to pray and think most carefully about your decisions.

13. In what ways does a footrace provide a helpful picture of the believer's life (Hebrews 12:1-3)? How might your incorporate Jesus' example into your prayers for yourself?

14. How is the harvest picture helpful in describing the believer's often difficult life (Galatians 6:9)? How will prayer help you remain faithful in spite of your stresses this week?

APPENDICES

TWENTY STEPS TO DAILY PRAYER

∽◎∾

In order to help you with a step-by-step approach to advancing your prayer life, consider the following suggested twenty-step guide. If you want to vary these to suit your schedule and preferences, please do so.

Each step represents one week. You may start with any step and progress onward from there (scan all preceding steps to benefit from practical pointers you might miss). It is better to start too low than too high. If you are not praying regularly, you are advised to start with Step 1.

A note about "failure": If, at any point, you fall short of your prayer goals for the week, don't let it defeat you. Forgive yourself and pick up where you left off. You may need to adjust your expectations or maintain a plateau for a while. In any case, remind yourself that you're probably praying more now than if you weren't making these efforts, and anticipate the rewards of your continued prayer growth (see Lesson 2).

Step 1

On the following scale, indicate the level of your current motivation to pray. Don't condemn yourself if your motivation is not where you want it to be. Accept yourself, and move on.

Motivation to Pray

1	2	3	4	5	6	7	8	9	10
Have to									**Want to**

Determine this week that every morning, when you wake in bed, you will say to God, perhaps silently, "I love You, Lord. This day is all about You and Your priorities." Tell Him something you appreciate about Him. (That's praise.) Determine to do the same thing each night when your head hits the pillow. Then do it as many days as you can remember to. A simple note attached to your alarm clock or mirror may help. I know of a pastor who gave each of his men a miniature bottle of Tabasco sauce. He instructed them to put it someplace where they would see it each morning (like the shower). It was to be a reminder to pray each morning that they would be "red hot" for God.

Step 2

Continue the morning and evening habit of checking in with God, and at one of those times—you choose, morning or evening—add a simple but meaningful request for some person or issue close to your heart, such as a family member or an important decision. This may be as short as one sentence, and it may be the same or different from day to day. Tell God your specific desire. Rather than a general, "Bless Sally," ask something like, "Help Sally to be patient with the kids today."

Step 3

Continue your daily prayer habit, this time expanding your time—either morning or evening—to two minutes each day, at least five days of the week. Choose a theme for your requests, something important to you, such as family or a significant need in your life.

If you run out of things to ask, simply think about God's presence, remaining silent or saying whatever comes to mind.

Start writing down your requests to help you remember them. You might simply use key words or phrases. Use any type of paper, cards, or notebook. (This is one type of prayer journaling.)

Step 4

Continue your daily prayer habit, this week praying three minutes a day, at least five days a week. Continue to write down your requests and to pray with your list available. Feel free still to focus on those people and needs most important to you.

Step 5

Increase your daily prayer time to five minutes a day, at least five days a week. If you prefer some time other than waking or bedtime, put it on your daily schedule and keep your appointments with God. You are encouraged to spend additional time praying each day while doing other tasks, such as driving or exercising.

Begin to include a limited number of requests for people or issues beyond those that are most important to you. You might pray for church and government leaders, needs in your church or community, unsaved acquaintances or relatives, or specific ministries and missionaries. Just choose a few specific requests, not everything.

Step 6

On the following scale, indicate the level of your current motivation to pray. Have you changed since Step 1? Even if you haven't, accept yourself, and move on.

Motivation to Pray

1	2	3	4	5	6	7	8	9	10
Have to								**Want to**	

Continue praying five minutes a day, at least five days a week. On one day, pray with someone else—your spouse, a child, a friend.

Step 7

Make it your goal to pray at least five minutes a day, all seven days this week. Pray one day with someone else, such as your spouse, a family member, or a friend. Keep writing down your requests.

Step 8

Continue praying five minutes a day, seven days a week. Continue writing down your requests.

Establish a weekly prayer appointment with another person. This appointment might be very short, but it needs to be a regular commitment to each other.

Step 9

Continue praying five minutes every day, and keep your weekly appointment with your prayer partner.

On one day, set aside fifteen minutes. Spend a few minutes reading from Scripture, then talking to God about what you've read (anything you've learned about Him, promises or instructions He has given you, sins to clear up with Him, and so on). If you need a passage to start with, try Psalm 33 or 34. Use the remainder of your time to pray as you usually do. This should be additional to any Bible reading program you may be going through.

Step 10

Continue praying five minutes every day, one day with your prayer partner.

On one day, set aside thirty minutes, using part of your time for Scripture reading, part for praying about what you have read, and part for praying as you do on other days. If you need some passages to start with, try Psalm 42-43, 63 or 77. This would be a good time to pray through all the lists you have written over the last several weeks. Consider also using the suggestions in Lesson 6, "What to Pray for People."

Ideas for Extended Prayer

While some people may have no trouble praying the same way for long periods of time, many of us need variety in order to keep our interest. Here are several ideas to consider:

1. Pray aloud, standing, moving around or with eyes open.
2. Sing a praise song or listen meditatively to recorded music, agreeing with and directing a song's ideas toward God.
3. Use visual reminders besides your prayer list, such as pictures of people, prayer letters, or news headlines.
4. You might find it helpful to structure your prayer time, as with the ACTS acrostic (Adoration, Confession, Thanksgiving, Supplication [requests]).
5. Use prayers in Scripture (such as Ephesians 1:17-19) as guides for some of your prayers, reciting a passage to God and inserting the names of people where appropriate.
6. Prepare ahead for your prayer sessions by gathering names, needs, and other information.

Step 11

Continue praying five minutes every day, one day with your prayer partner.

Some time this week, set aside an hour for prayer and prayerful Scripture reading (consider using Psalms 86, 91, 92, 95-97). Pray through lists from the past several weeks. Pray on a variety of topics, including those listed under Step 5. Allow times of silence, submitting your heart to God's guidance, simply recognizing His presence, accepting His love.

Especially during silent times, you may think of possible steps of action and obedience you could take in your life (some as simple as, "Apologize to Fred," some as substantial as, "Begin lifelong Bible memory program"). Start writing these down as possible goals as they come to mind. Make this a regular habit during prayer, creating a fresh list each day or week. Don't stop to evaluate your goals as you pray; keep praying. But come back to them at least one day later, and reconsider which, if any, of these would be important for you to pursue. When the time comes to take action, start with short, easy-to-reach goals. Allow yourself much more time (weeks) to evaluate long-term goals.

Step 12

On the following scale, indicate the level of your current motivation to pray. Have you changed since Step 6? Even if you haven't, accept yourself, and move on.

Motivation to Pray

1	2	3	4	5	6	7	8	9	10
Have to								**Want to**	

Follow the instructions in Step 11. Repeating the same pattern will help solidify the gains you have made in your prayer life. Focus on enjoying the Lord who is there with you. Remember that He enjoys your company and that He hears every request.

Some time this week, take a few minutes to read any tentative goals you wrote down on last week's new goal list. Prayerfully decide on one or two new goals you want to pursue, or continue with goals you are already implementing.

Step 13

Increase your daily prayer time to ten minutes. Start the habit of keeping your open Bible in front of you, allowing God to speak to you through His Word as you read for at least a minute or two. Consider selections from Psalms 98-100, 103, 104. Continue to write down your prayer requests and any tentative goals that come to mind.

Keep meeting weekly with your prayer partner. Start sharing with each other one or two growth goals you have decided on. Do this each week, checking up on past goals. Don't let your list get too long (between three and ten is plenty, including your prayer goals).

Set aside one continuous hour for prayer, as in Steps 11 and 12.

Prayerfully review your previous week's new tentative goal list, and decide on any new goals you want to pursue.

Step 14

Increase your prayer time to a cumulative fifteen minutes each day. This might be all in one session, or broken up into two or more sessions throughout the day. You are also encouraged to spend additional time praying while you go about your daily tasks.

Keep meeting weekly with your prayer partner.

Set aside one continuous hour for prayer some time during the week.

Prayerfully review your previous week's new tentative goal list, and decide on any new goals you want to pursue.

Step 15

Maintain a cumulative fifteen minutes of prayer each day.

Keep meeting weekly with your prayer partner.

Set aside one continuous hour for prayer some time during the week, and choose another day when you will pray for a cumulative hour, either as a continuous session or broken up into smaller portions throughout the day.

Prayerfully review your previous week's goal list, and decide on any new goals you want to pursue.

Step 16

Pray a cumulative twenty minutes each day.

Keep meeting weekly with your prayer partner.

Set aside one continuous hour for prayer some time during the week, and choose another day when you will pray for a cumulative hour, either as a continuous session or broken up into smaller portions throughout the day.

Prayerfully review your previous week's goal list, and decide on any new goals you want to pursue.

Step 17

Pray a cumulative thirty minutes each day.

Keep meeting weekly with your prayer partner.

Set aside one continuous hour for prayer some time during the week, and choose another day when you will pray for a cumulative hour.

Prayerfully review your previous week's goal list, and decide on any new goals you want to pursue.

If you've found yourself making sporadic progress up to this point, you may choose to maintain this level of prayer commitment for several weeks or months before advancing to Step 18 and beyond.

Step 18

On the following scale, indicate the level of your current motivation to pray. Have you changed since Step 12? Even if you haven't, accept yourself, and move on.

Motivation to Pray

1	2	3	4	5	6	7	8	9	10
Have to									**Want to**

Pray a cumulative forty minutes each day.

Keep meeting weekly with your prayer partner.

Set aside two separate one-hour prayer sessions this week.

Prayerfully review your previous week's goal list, and decide on any new goals you want to pursue.

Step 19

Pray a cumulative fifty minutes each day.

Keep meeting weekly with your prayer partner.

Set aside two separate one-hour prayer sessions this week.

Prayerfully review your previous week's goal list, and decide on any new goals you want to pursue.

Step 20

Increase your daily prayer commitment to a cumulative hour per day. Pray also throughout the day, while doing other tasks, but carefully guard your daily portion of undistracted prayer.

Choose at least two days when your hour of prayer will be continuous and uninterrupted.

Keep meeting weekly with your prayer partner.

Prayerfully review your previous week's goal list.

Appendix B

HELP!
I'M DROWNING!

$\sim\!\!\text{\reflectbox{Q}}\!\!\sim$

If, at any point in this study, you have begun to feel overwhelmed and to despair of ever being able to live up to the disciplines we've described, then this appendix is for you. We know that anyone can learn the discipline of prayer. God has placed the habit of prayer within the reach of every one of His children, just as every good-hearted parent desires to keep avenues of communication open with his or her children. If you are experiencing fear or hopelessness about your prayer life, let's take a little break from the studies and discuss one possible reason for your discouragement.

When God's Word challenges us, we sometimes discover that we lack the hope needed to respond with courageous obedience. One outstanding destroyer of hope and courage is a history of life experiences that has simply drained off the vital energy needed to maintain hope. For most of us, when we first became believers, we started out with high expectations based on God's promises. But then life happened. Financial hardships, relational disasters, dissatisfying careers, deaths of loved ones, negative church encounters, and a host of other experiences have sent many of us into a downward spiral that might even be labeled outright depression—or at least deep discouragement.

Bogged down in this emotional mire, you may find it extremely difficult to muster any energy to take a risk of obedience. You have probably taken some of those risks before, and you may have been burned and hurt to the point that you've vowed never to take any risks again. Your dreams have died, you've grieved their loss, and you've now settled into a malaise in which you hope just to endure the rest of your years without serious pain. The challenges of Scripture presented in these studies may meet with apathy or strike fear in your heart.

If this describes your current emotional and spiritual condition to some degree, you may find solace in knowing that you're not alone. Take comfort also in the knowledge that God stills loves you and has somehow provided a way out of your emotional dungeon (1 Corinthians 10:13).

I encourage you to talk with a pastor or a trusted, mature believing friend. A person who can ask questions and help discern your unique set of needs can best help you learn to hope and dream again. Also, because there are some characteristics common to many people in this position, we offer a few suggestions that may prove helpful.

First, let us dispel a misconception about prayer—namely, that effective prayer must be based on "strong faith" and that you must come to God with a power of conviction before you can pray effectively. In fact, prayer is, in its essence, an expression of our own helplessness and need to depend on God. God's favorite prayer is simply, "Help!"

God honors faith. But, rather than being some strength we build up, faith can just as much be displayed through our helpless dependence on the strength of God. So if you are feeling helpless, weak—even worthless—you're in the best position to send up a genuine prayer of totally dependent faith to God. You, of all people, know you can't rescue yourself and are ready to see God work miracles that could only be from Him.

Second, don't set early expectations of yourself too high (even the minimal expectations established in this book may be too high for some people at the start). Set yourself up for small, early victories by establishing meaningful, but reachable, goals. If you are so discouraged about life that you feel defeated by the idea of an hour of prayer a day, then plan for ten or fifteen minutes. Focus those prayers on the issues you are passionate about. They will most likely raise some energy and interest in your weary heart. For example, most people will do well simply to start praying for family, or others closest to them.

By choosing a short-term, reachable goal, you make it much more likely that you'll be celebrating a small victory soon (such as maintaining your habit daily for a week). Then use the growing ember of hope from that victory to fuel your progress on toward a slightly higher and riskier goal. And remember, your growth in confidence and faithfulness is the real victory. God, in His wisdom, may not answer your prayers the way you expect, so don't use outward circumstances to measure success.

Third, recognize that life will still continue to present you with disappointments, and that some of your risks of obedience will not "pay off" as you might hope. This is normal, and God has promised the grace to help you endure disappointments. As you persevere in His strength and love, your eventual victories and successes will dwarf the disappointments. The obedient life is risky, but, in God's universe, obedience is always an affordable risk.

Fourth, as a last resort, consider consulting a medical doctor to see if there may be some physiological component to your discouragement. If there is, it doesn't mean that you're "broken." It's quite common for long-term stress to deplete important chemicals in the body's nervous system, causing temporary depression. That can be corrected if the body and spirit are given the right kind of emotional and physical resources for restoration. God has created us as integrated beings. Our bodies, minds, and emotions work together as an interlinked whole. Because of this, there's absolutely no shame in recognizing a physical contributor or a partial physical solution to a spiritual and emotional problem.

Finally, above all else, seek God as a Father—not a senile, marshmallow of a grandfather, nor a dictatorial ogre, but a wise Father who loves you with both truth and grace. He's a Father you can trust, and if you approach Him consistently with a desire to learn to trust Him, He will change you, releasing you from your fears by showing you gradually who He really is, entrusting you with His own vulnerable, open heart. He's been burned, too, and He knows how it feels. He welcomes even your feeble, early efforts, and He understands and forgives your weaknesses. He longs for your company even more than you long for His. He treasures you enough that He paid for you with His Son. Indeed, you can learn to trust a Father like that.

Appendix C

HELP!
I'M STUCK!

∿☙∿

The preceding appendix addressed those who feel overwhelmed by prayer. However, you may instead find yourself unable to get past a barrier of apathy. Maybe you're stopped at the starting gate, not really wanting to begin. Or perhaps you've progressed several steps in your prayer life, but you're not finding motivation to go further.

One reason for this might be that you have failed to keep up with your prayer goals, so you feel you must make up ground, or accomplish some other feat of penance to gain God's acceptance before progressing. Failure may feel like an insurmountable mountain range. But failure becomes a friend when we choose to see it as a learning opportunity, allowing us to move ahead with greater wisdom. Don't play catch up, and don't beat yourself up. If your expectations were too high, adjust them. But even if they weren't, please accept God's forgiveness, forgive yourself, and move on.

Another common hindrance to prayer is fear of intimacy. Perhaps deeper commitment to prayer threatens you, because it would mean baring your soul before God or before another person. This can be extremely intimidating to many people, especially those who tend to be more reserved. But even some who are generally outgoing may have compartments of their inner selves that they're afraid to reveal.

If you are threatened by fear of intimacy, you may not even recognize what is happening within you. You won't tend to actively resist the threat (in this case, prayer), but you may respond with passive aggression—resisting the threatening activity through non-cooperation, rather than lashing out. Resistance may express itself through the excuse that it takes too long to get emotionally "ready" to pray, and so there is never time to pray "the right way" or "with the right attitude."

An outside observer may even assume you're just stubborn. You know your heart's desire is to do the right thing, but that desire is deadened by paralysis and lethargy, rooted in fear.

Lack of motivation to pray is closely related to being overwhelmed as discussed in Appendix B, so you will probably benefit from reading that as well. Also, here are a few steps to consider if you face a wall of apathy.

First, ask God for a growing passion and love for Him. Even if you make this your only prayer request for weeks to come, ask for this. When God stirs your heart to the point that longing for Him overwhelms your fear, then you'll find the momentum to overcome the barriers inside you (see Lesson 7; also Jeremiah 29:13).

Second, "Taste and see that the Lord is good" (Psalm 34:8). God invites us to take Him at His word that He can be trusted. When we simply act on His promises, over time He creates within us confidence, joy, security, and passion. Act on faith and "go through the motions" if you must. Sometimes behavior precedes feelings. Don't wait until you feel like praying. Just pray. Then, in time, you will experience the emotional fruit of God's Spirit rewarding you inwardly (Galatians 5:22-23).

Third, consider possible misconceptions you may believe about prayer. For example, do you buy into the fallacy that prayer must always be done in a certain place and posture, eyes closed, hands folded? Certainly we must guard time for undistracted prayer. But God is with us all day long, and He enjoys our ongoing conversation with Him even while we're driving, working, eating, talking, or dealing with a crisis. All of these are good times to talk with Him, even if it's a quick word or two.

Other misconceptions include the idea that we can't go to God with an impure heart (how else to purify our hearts, but to confess the impurity to God?); that we must drum up a certain level of "reverence" before praying (often reverence grows as we pray, not before); or that prayer is a fruitless waste of time (what greater use of time than to call on the God of the universe to act in His own best interest?). Some other mistaken ways of thinking about prayer are addressed throughout the lessons in this book.

Fourth, examine your heart to see what you are living for. What do you spend the most time, money, and effort pursuing throughout your week? What are your affections set upon? There are many possibilities besides God—wealth, influence, toys, convenience, pleasure, and so on. None of these, in iself, is necessarily evil. But evaluate whether God has been displaced by something else at the center of your heart. If so, then it is no wonder you have difficulty mustering passion for Him.

What do you do if you discover such an intruder? Ask God to change your heart. And ask someone you trust for help (see Lesson 10). It isn't easy to change your heart's affections, especially when you've set them on an unworthy object for a long time. Asking for help is humbling, but it can be extremely rewarding. Consider going to a mature friend or a trusted leader.

These thoughts may help you begin both to do the right things (grow in your prayer habit) and to do them for the right reasons (primarily out of love for God). Even if it takes some time for you to address the emotional needs you find within yourself, take that time. You may not yet be prepared to run the "prayer marathon" you see some others running. But by taking seriously your need for emotional and spiritual healing and growth, at whatever stage you find yourself, you'll soon discover new motivation and passion, and your fears will fade. You'll be discovering the Father you can trust with your life and everything in it.

Appendix D

PERSONALITY ASSESSMENT GUIDE

∽ↀ∾

In conjunction with Lesson 5, the following guidelines are intended to help you evaluate your own personality traits that impact your style of prayer. Try to be realistic and objective about yourself, assessing the ways you normally think and behave. Try to avoid choosing traits you wish you had, but can't truly justify. Once you have attained a more accurate understanding of your personality, you will be better able to capitalize on your strengths and to strengthen your weaknesses.

For each pair of traits, mark on the scale where you estimate your personality falls. You might ask a friend or family member to help you by circling the key words that best describe you. Encourage them to be honest.

A. **Optimistic** 3　2　1　0　1　2　3　**Solemn**

　　Happy-go-lucky　　　　　　　　　　**Sober minded**
　　Focuses on positive　　　　　　　　**Focuses on negative**

Optimistic. To this person, life's struggles are seen as blessings in disguise. This person's prayers are usually positive. However, a solemn person may view an optimistic person as a naive or "surface" individual.

Solemn. This trait anticipates the negative forces that shape our lives and tends to focus on such themes as fear, hate, violence, pain, and discouragement. His prayers emphasize seriously needy individuals and problematic events. This trait may doubt that God's power can overcome worldly forces. For those who are strong in this trait, consistently focusing on the Person of Almighty God is recommended.

B. **Assertive** 3 2 1 0 1 2 3 **Submissive**

Decisive   Compliant

Demands own way   Gives in to pressure

Assertive. An extremely assertive person is domineering, like Hitler and Stalin. Healthier expressions of assertiveness include taking charge, being proactive, and exhibiting decisiveness. This person is willing and able to make necessary decisions when another's feelings may get ruffled. He or she tends to be forthright with intentions.

Submissive. The Bible endorses submissiveness as a virtue, not to be confused with passivity or reluctance to commit. It involves a conscious, daily practice of subordinating one's self-interest to God's desires. Nonbiblical "submission" may express itself as indifference, inaction, failure to confront evil or sin and reluctance to give a clear "no" or "yes." Those who are more compliant or passive find it harder to claim God's promises and to make commitments requiring a price. Careful understanding of biblical submission, as opposed to passivity, is important in developing an active prayer life.

C. **Subjective** 3 2 1 0 1 2 3 **Objective**

Feeling-oriented   Fact-oriented

decision making   decision making

Subjective. Generally artists, musicians, and those with a flair for acting and drama, tend to be subjective in their approach to life. This means buying a car or a house is an act of the emotions. The right choice "feels good." Sometimes, in extreme cases, the emotions overrule common sense. This person's prayers will usually carry emotional depth and fervor. He or she is encouraged to grow in balance and tolerance toward those who are more objective and appear to be indifferent or "cold fish."

Objective. This trait, carried to its extreme, trusts only cold, hard facts, giving no credence to the "heart" or passion. The objective trait is first driven to look at the proven or known data. This trait may find it difficult to look beyond the known facts, to dwell on the possibilities of passion and faith. This person must be cautious about the danger of rejecting those who are more driven by feelings.

D. **Expressive** 3   2   1   0   1   2   3   Reserved

Open   **Discreet**

Shares inner feelings   **Private**

Expressive. This trait, in its extreme, wears its heart on its sleeve. One of this person's weaknesses is a lack of discretion, a failure to distinguish between what is appropriate and what is inappropriate to share with others. This trait, in healthy moderation, brings a sweet openness and honesty to relationships. It doesn't hide or pretend. This person may tend to think negatively and critically of others who are more private and reserved in group prayer. Most often this person will be as open with God in prayer as with other people.

Reserved. This trait is reluctant to share deep thoughts or emotions, sometimes even in a close relationship. Often the fear of sharing with others is paralleled by a reluctance to share openly with God. This person is encouraged to frequently ask God to help develop trust and openness with Him—a habit that will help a reserved person make the most of this study. Those who are more reserved need to guard against critical thoughts toward those who pray openly about their deep needs.

E. **Spontaneous** 3   2   1   0   1   2   3   Persevering

Spur of the moment   **Goal-oriented**

Impulsive   **Disciplined**

Spontaneous. This trait is quick to become excited or to express passion. In group prayer, a spontaneous person contributes a spark of intensity that stimulates others to join in. But this person may also lose interest in a project when the going gets tough. He or she tends to feel intense enthusiasm in the early stages, but becomes distracted by new ventures when the original project reaches the follow-through and maintenance phases.

Persevering. A persevering person is strongly self-disciplined and goal-oriented. He or she will persist in prayer for the long haul. This person is easily irritated by the on-and-off nature of the spontaneous temperament. He or she tends not to become easily excited or to react with intensity to an immediate need. This can be positive in that it exercises discretion, but may also be negative when the need is genuine and requires quick response. Individuals with this trait are usually the reliable prayer warriors.

These five personality trait categories were selected because they tend to impact one's style and approach to prayer more dramatically than other traits. As you can see, balance and tolerance are key. Pray for yourself and for those who are distinctly different from you, that we might together function as the healthy body God desires.

SAMPLE ACCOUNTABILITY GOAL LIST

⚬⚭⚬

This is the list used by the "E-Men," an accountability group marked by weekly email updates and a monthly breakfast meeting, at Jefferson Baptist Church. These goals are ones we derived to be accountable for to each other. They are only presented here as samples of what one men's group did. Please do not just adapt them for your group. If God has not given them to you, they will just be legalistic for your group.

1. Participate in two church corporate prayer meetings each month.

2. Pray with your spouse two times each week. Saying grace at meals or similar prayer times don't count. This needs to be a significant time.

3. Memorize one verse each week. Put these on 3x5 cards and bring them to the monthly breakfast.

4. Read ten chapters in the Bible each week. You should have some Bible reading plan that you are working through.

5. Greet one person you don't know in church each week. Get their name and include it in your weekly email report.

6. Make a list of seven lost people and pray for them weekly.

7. Read twenty pages every week from a good, Bible-based book.

8. Establish personal goals for yourself, different from these corporate goals. Write them down; then read those goals at least once each week.

9. Be faithful to attend the men's breakfast each month, being sure to bring your verses and your personal goals to report on your progress.

10. Email the men in your group every week, even if you did poorly at reaching your goals.

11. Faithfully pray for each of the men in your group as you read their reports. Praying as you read the reports will ensure you will do it. Try to send prayer requests with each of your weekly reports, and respond to each other's emails.

12. Be honest and transparent—no "smoke blowing."

Appendix F

SPIRITUAL WARFARE

~◎~

1. Angels are God's servants who are doing much of His work on this earth at His command. (Genesis 28:12; Exodus 23:20; Psalm 91:11-12, 103:20-21; Daniel 6:22, 7:9-10; Zechariah 1:9-10; Matthew 4:11, 18:10, 24:31, 28:2-3; Luke 1:19, 15:10, 16:22, 22:41-43; Acts 5:18-20; Hebrews 1:14, 13:2; Revelation 5:11-12, 7:1-3,11-12, 10:1-3, 19:17)

2. The demons of Satan are resisting and fighting against the angels of God and against believers. (Daniel 10:20-21; Revelation 12:7)

3. Satan and his demons have a great deal of influence and power in this world. (Luke 4:5-6; 2 Corinthians 4:4; Ephesians 6:11-12; 2 Timothy 2:26)

4. The outcome of the spiritual battle determines, to a great extent, the course of events in the physical world. (Exodus 17:9-13)

5. When we pray, God commissions His angels to accomplish His will. (Numbers 20:16; Isaiah 37:15,21,36; Daniel 9:21-23, 10:11-12; Acts 10:3-4, 12:7-12)

6. When we pray, God energizes His angels to overcome all resistance to the accomplishment of God's will. (Psalm 35:1, 5-6; Daniel 10:13; Revelation 12:7-8)

7. The failure to pray creates a spiritual energy crisis that allows the kingdom of evil to prevail in our world.

Appendix G

QUOTES ON GOALS AND GOAL SETTING

~_ᐤ~

"The failure to set goals is the main cause of mediocrity in the Christian life." (Larry Crabb)

"Everything we do is in response to a goal we are trying to accomplish. A problem we have, though, is that we haven't identified our goals in a firm, conscious way. Instead, they are general, wandering thoughts that change regularly. Each of us goes through life responding to his or her goals. We may not call them 'goals,' but that is what they are. How we are living at any moment is determined by the goal toward which we are moving. Everything we do is motivated by a goal we have." (Ed Dayton and Ted Engstrom)

"Man is functionally like a bicycle. Unless he's moving onward and upward towards an objective—a goal—he's going to falter and fall." (Maxwell Maltz)

"Give me a stock clerk with a goal and I will give you a man who will make history. Give me a man without a goal, and I will give you a stock clerk." (J. C. Penney)

"People are designed for lives of richness and challenge. We were made for achievement and fulfillment. It was not intended that our lives be boring, or constantly frustrating, or dominated by failure. We were made for reaching and stretching. We were designed with the physical and emotional equipment to be constantly in a state of change and improvement. Everything about us as people indicates an almost limitless capacity for variety and positive growth." (Charles Paul Conn)

"There is a false assumption on the part of many pastors that only a few are gifted with vision. According to their way of thinking, some have it, others don't. However, this would mean God has a dream and plan for some churches, but not for others. That makes no sense at all." (Dr. Henry Klopp)

"The world of the 1990s and beyond will not belong to 'managers' or those who can make the numbers dance. The world will belong to passionate, driven leaders—people who not only have enormous amounts of energy but who can energize those whom they lead." (Jack Welch, CEO of General Electric)

"Do not underestimate the power and importance of a dream. It will be impossible for your church to get out of its holding pattern without a dream. Someone must have vision of the good, the wonderful, and the possible that is in the future of your church. . . . Dream big dreams. You can never achieve more than someone dares to dream." (Charles Chaney and Ron Lewis)

"There is no more powerful engine driving an organization toward excellence and long-range success than an attractive, worthwhile, and achievable vision of the future, widely shared." (Burt Nanus)

"The most important problem in the church today is a fundamental lack of clear, heart-grabbing vision. It has programs and institutions and property and ministers and politically correct hymnals, but no vision." (Mike Regale)

"Success is accomplishing the goals that God has led me to set." (Charles Stanley)

"Leaders, like artists, attempt to create extraordinary new realities out of ordinary materials through the force of vision." (Burt Nanus)

"Great leadership requires a great vision, one that inspires the leader and inspires him to inspire the nation. People both love and hate the great leader; they are seldom indifferent toward him." (Richard Nixon)

"Leaders express the values, the vision, the culture that holds the organization together, goals to lift people out of their petty occupations, above their interpersonal conflicts, and unite them in pursuit of objectives worthy of their best efforts. Human behavior in an organization is very much shaped by a shared vision of a better tomorrow. Developing and promulgating such vision is the highest calling and truest purpose of leadership, for people instinctively 'follow the fellow who follows the dream.'" (John Gardner)

"People seem to need and want something they can commit to, a significant challenge worthy of their best efforts." (Burt Nanus)

"Selecting and articulating the right vision, this powerful idea, is the toughest task and the truest test of great leadership." (Burt Nanus)

"The greatest force for the advancement of the human species is a great hope held in common." (Burt Nanus)

"There is no mystery about it. Effective leaders adopt challenging new visions of what is both possible and desirable, communicate their visions, and persuade others to become so committed to these new directions that they are eager to lend their resources and energies to make them happen. After the completion of Disney World, someone remarked, 'Isn't it too bad that Walt Disney didn't live to see this!' Mike Vance, creative director of Disney Studios replied, 'He did see it—that's why it's here.'" (Burt Nanus)

"Not much happens without a dream. And for something great to happen there must always be a great dream. Behind every great achievement is a dreamer of great dreams. Much more than a dream is required to bring it to reality; but the dream must be there first." (Robert Greenleaf)

"Vision is the art of seeing things invisible." (Jonathan Swift)

"You are always casting and communicating vision. It is not an activity; it is a lifestyle. It is not something you put into your Day Timer. It is the way you live." (Jim Dethmer)

"More failures in the church come about because of an ambiguity of purpose than for any other reason." (Howard Hendricks)

"Without question, communicating the vision, and the atmosphere around the vision, has been, and is continuing to be, by far the toughest job we face. . . . You don't get anywhere if you keep changing your ideas. The only way to change people's minds is with consistency. Once you get the ideas, you keep refining and improving them; the more simply your idea is defined the better it is. You communicate, you communicate, and then you communicate some more. Consistency, simplicity, and repetition is what it's all about." (Jack Welch, CEO of General Electric)

"The far greater problem is when no one has made the effort to define success in advance. Without a well-defined target, it is hard to determine if someone is a winner even if he or she hits the bull's eye every time. . . . Some individuals and organizations balk at the notion of defining success in advance—especially churches. Some believe there is a lack of spirituality about such definitions. The reality is that all persons and organizations define success whether they admit to it or not." (Leith Anderson)

Scripture is much more inspiring and direction giving than any of these quotes

Appendix H

ADDITIONAL RESOURCES ON PRAYER

∽◎∼

Aldrich, Joe. *Reunitus—Building Bridges to Each Other Through Prayer Summits.* Sisters, OR: Multnomah Press, 1992.

Barna, George. *Today's Pastors.* Ventura, CA: Regal Books, 1993.

Billheimer, Paul E. *Destined for the Throne.* Minneapolis: Bethany, 1975. X

Bonar, Andrew A., ed. *Memoirs of McCheyne.* Chicago: Moody Press, 1844.

Bounds, E. M. *The Essentials of Prayer.* Grand Rapids, MI: Baker, 1990.

_____. *The Necessity of Prayer.* Grand Rapids, MI: Baker, 1976.

_____. *Power through Prayer.* Grand Rapids, MI: Zondervan, 1962. X

_____. *Powerful and Prayerful Pulpits.* Grand Rapids, MI: Baker, 1993.

_____. *Prayer and Praying Men.* Grand Rapids, MI: Baker, 1977.

_____. *The Weapon of Prayer.* Grand Rapids, MI: Baker, 1975.

Brase, Lee. *Approaching God: Lessons from the Inspired Prayers of Scripture.* Colorado Springs, CO: NavPress, 2003.

Bright, Bill. *The Coming Revival—America's Call to Fast, Pray, and "Seek God's Face."* Orlando: New Life Publications, 1995.

Bryant, David. *How Christians Can Join Together in Concerts of Prayer.* Ventura, CA: Regal, 1984.

Chafer, Lewis Sperry. *True Evangelism—Winning Souls by Prayer.* Grand Rapids, MI: Zondervan, 1919.

Curran, Sue. *The Praying Church: Principles and Power of Corporate Praying.* Blountville, TN: Shekinah Publishing, 1987.

Cymbala, Jim. *Breakthrough Prayer.* Grand Rapids, MI: Zondervan Publishing House, 2003.

_____. *Fresh Wind, Fresh Fire.* Grand Rapids, MI: Zondervan Publishing House, 1997.

Dean, Jennifer Kennedy. *Live a Praying Life: Open Your Life to God's Power and Provision.* Birmingham, AL: New Hope Publishers, 2003.

Gesswein, Armin R. *With One Accord In One Place.* Harrisburg, PA: Christian Publications, 1978.

Graf, Jonathan and Lani Hinkle, eds. *My House Shall Be a House of Prayer.* Colorado Springs, CO: NavPress, 2001.

Graf, Jonathan. *The Power of Personal Prayer: Learning to Pray with Faith and Purpose.* Colorado Springs, CO: NavPress, 2002.

Grenz, Stanley J. *Prayer: The Cry for the Kingdom.* Peabody, MA: Hendrickson Publishing, 1988.

Grubb, Norman. *Rees Howells, Intercessor.* Fort Washington, PA: Christian Literature Crusade, 1954.

Hall, Robert, ed. *Charles Spurgeon—The Power of Prayer in a Believer's Life*. Lynnwood, WA: Emerald Books, 1993.

Hallesby, O. *Prayer*. Minneapolis: Augsburg, 1931.

Hartley, Fred A., III. *Lord, Teach Us to Pray: Finding Delight in the Practice of Prayer*. Colorado Springs, CO: NavPress, 2003.

Henderson, Dr. Daniel. *Fresh Encounters: Meeting God through United Worship-based Prayer*. Colorado Springs, CO: NavPress, 2004.

Long, Brad, and Doug McMurry. *Prayer That Shapes the Future: How to Pray with Power and Authority*. Grand Rapids, MI: Zondervan Publishing House, 1999.

Martin, Glen and Dian Ginter. *Power House—Step-by-Step Guide to Building a Church that Prays*. Nashville: Broadman & Holman Publishing, 1994.

Murray, Andrew. *The Ministry of Intercession—A Plea for More Prayer*. New York: Revel, 1897.

_____. *With Christ in the School of Prayer*. New York: Revel, 1985.

Ridings, Dean. *The Pray! Prayer Journal: Daily Steps Toward Praying God's Heart*. Colorado Springs, CO: NavPress, 2003.

Sack, Cheryl. *The Prayer Saturated Church: A Comprehensive Handbook for Prayer Leaders*. Colorado Springs, CO: NavPress, 2004.

Searle, Walter, ed. *David Brainard's Personal Testimony*. Grand Rapids, MI: Baker, 1978.

Taylor, Dr. and Mrs. Howard. *Hudson Taylor's Spiritual Secret*. Chicago: Moody Press, 1932.

Wagner, C. Peter. *Churches That Pray: How Prayer Can Help Revitalize Your Congregation and Break Down the Walls Between Your Church and Your Community*. Ventura, CA: Regal, 1993.

White, Tom. *The Believer's Guide to Spiritual Warfare*. Ann Arbor, MI: Servant Publications, 1990.

_____. *City-Wide Prayer Movements: One Church, Many Congregations*. Ann Arbor, MI: Servant Publications, 2001.

Willard, Dallas. *The Spirit of the Disciplines*. San Francisco: Harper & Row, 1988.

Winger, Dr. Mell, ed. *Fight on Your Knees: Calling Men to Action through Transforming Prayer*. Colorado Springs, CO: NavPress 2002.